Best Easy Day Hikes
Capitol Reef National Park

Help Us Keep This Guide Up to Date

Every effort has been made by the author and editors to make this guide as accurate and useful as possible. However, many things can change after a guide is published—trails are rerouted, regulations change, techniques evolve, facilities come under new management, etc.

We would appreciate hearing from you concerning your experiences with this guide and how you feel it could be improved and kept up to date. While we may not be able to respond to all comments and suggestions, we will take them to heart, and we will also make certain to share them with the authors. Please send your comments and suggestions to the following address:

Globe Pequot
Reader Response/Editorial Department
246 Goose Lane
Guilford, CT 06437

Or you may e-mail us at:

editorial@falcon.com

Thanks for your input, and happy trails!

Best Easy Day Hikes Series

Best Easy Day Hikes
Capitol Reef
National Park

Brett Prettyman

FALCONGUIDES

GUILFORD, CONNECTICUT
HELENA, MONTANA

FALCONGUIDES®

An imprint of Globe Pequot
Falcon, FalconGuides, and Make Adventure Your Story are registered
trademarks of Rowman & Littlefield.

Distributed by NATIONAL BOOK NETWORK

Copyright © 2017 by Rowman & Littlefield

Maps by Alena Pearce © Rowman & Littlefield

British Library Cataloguing-in-Publication Information available

Library of Congress Cataloging-in-Publication Data available

ISBN 978-1-4930-2647-0 (paperback)
ISBN 978-1-4930-2648-7 (e-book)

∞ ™ The paper used in this publication meets the minimum requirements
of American National Standard for Information Sciences—Permanence
of Paper for Printed Library Materials, ANSI/NISO Z39.48-1992.

Printed in the United States of America

Contents

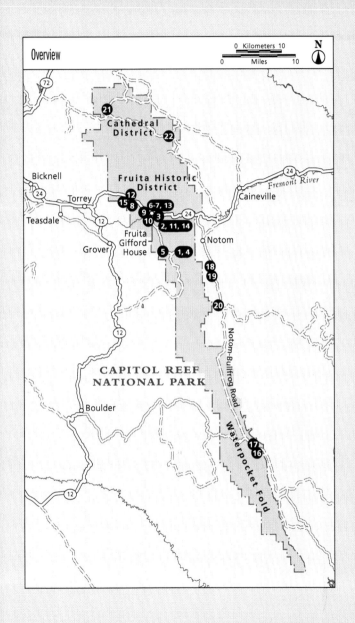

Overview

0 ─── Kilometers ─── 10
0 ─── Miles ─── 10

N

72

21
Cathedral
District

22

Bicknell

24 Torrey

Teasdale

12

Grover

Fruita Historic
District

12
15 8

Fruita
Gifford
House

9 6-7, 13
10 3
2, 11, 14

5

1, 4

24

24 Fremont River

Caineville

Notom

18
19

20

CAPITOL REEF
NATIONAL PARK

Boulder

12

Notom-Bullfrog Road

Waterpocket Fold

17
16

Acknowledgments

Thanks to the staff and volunteers at Capitol Reef National Park for providing vital and accurate details on the hikes in the book. Few people love the parks more than those who make a living in them, and I appreciate their desire to share the wonders of Capitol Reef with the public. Special thanks to Capitol Reef Superintendent Leah McGinnis, Chief of Interpretation Cindy Micheli, and Chief of Resource Management and Science Terry Fisk. If you are looking for deeper details on the hikes in this book and options for longer adventures, make sure to check out Capitol Reef National Park volunteer Rick Stinchfield's book *Capitol Reef National Park: The Complete Hiking and Touring Guide.* Thanks to my good friend Vince Horiuchi for technical help.

Introduction

Capitol Reef is the least visited of Utah's five national parks. With no lodge in the park and limited hotel rooms in nearby towns, many international tourists leave the Reef off of their must-see list when traveling to Utah. That is just fine with those who have found the park and hope it will remain forever off the beaten path, so they can find alone time on the trails of Capitol Reef. That being said, the park flirts with one million visitors each year. The name came from early Mormon settlers who thought the white domes of Navajo sandstone in the area looked like the Capitol building in Washington, D.C. The Reef portion of the name came from prospectors, some perhaps with sailing experience, who felt the Waterpocket Fold—a 100-mile long ridge on the east side of the park—looked like a large barrier reef in the desert. Capitol Reef was first designated as a national monument in 1937. The highway reached Fruita in 1952, making it possible for more visitors to make the journey. Eventually, the National Park Service decided to buy all property still privately owned. Capitol Reef became a national park in December of 1971 when President Richard Nixon signed a bill.

Ancient People

Long before the first Mormon pioneers visited the area that came to be known as Capitol Reef, there were people who called it home. Archaeologists refer to the artifacts found in the area as being from the Fremont Culture. The Fremont are believed to have been hunter/gatherers who augmented their diet of local wildlife and native plants by planting corn, beans, and squash along what would come to be known as the Fremont River.

The Fremont people are believed to have frequented the area from about AD 600–1300. Pictographs and petroglyphs believed to have been created during that time frame can be found throughout the national park. There is an easily accessible and large panel of this rock art located along Hwy. 24, a mile east of the visitor center. Visitors can walk along a boardwalk to see the people, wildlife, and abstract images on Wingate sandstone cliffs. Binoculars enhance the viewing experience.

Fruita

The Fruita Historic District is the heart of Capitol Reef National Park. The stretch of Hwy. 24 in the Fruita area includes the visitor center, the Fruita Schoolhouse, and the petroglyph panel. The road from the visitor center to the scenic drive includes the Ripple Rock Nature Center, a blacksmith shop, a picnic area, and the Gifford homestead. A little farther on the road and visitors with plans to spend the night in the park will find the campground. The amphitheater used for ranger programs is also located near the campground.

Visitors will also notice a plethora of trees—not just trees, but fruit trees—the basis of the name Fruita for the community near the junction of the Fremont River and Sulphur Creek.

While explorers and settlers had ventured through the area before, the first recognized modern inhabitant of what would become Fruita did not arrive until 1879. Nels Johnson became the first landholder in what was then known as Junction. The name Fruita was adopted in 1902. Historians note the population of the community never exceeded more than ten families and the last family officially left in 1969.

The fruit orchards, however, remain. Capitol Reef is one of only a few national park units in the United States to offer fresh-off-the-tree fruit for visitors and in some of the most scenic red rock country in the world, no less.

Park officials say there are approximately 3,100 trees in nineteen Capitol Reef orchards including apple, cherry, peach, pear, apricot, plum, and mulberry. Almond and walnut trees are also found in the national park orchards.

The orchards, some of which are located near the campground, are open to the public when park officials deem the fruit or nuts ready for collection. Casual picking is free and campers often stroll through the nearby orchards for a naturally sweet treat. Collecting larger amounts requires a self-pay process based on weight, and commercial harvest requires a permit.

Of special note is the fact that one of the more than two dozen varieties of apples found in the Utah national park is one unique to the planet.

The Capitol Reef Red was recognized as a distinct variety in 1994. Capitol Reef Red apples can be found in the Jackson Orchard.

Some people, my family included, plan their trips to Capitol Reef during blooming or harvest seasons. Seeing the orchards in full bloom alongside the red cliff walls of the Utah desert is stunning. Picking fruit from those same orchards months later is just as unique.

Park officials provide the following time charts for visitor reference, but keep in mind that Mother Nature sometimes challenges the range.

Flowering Range
    Cherries—Mar 31–Apr 19
    Apricots—Feb 27–Mar 20 (early) and Mar 7–Apr 13 (regular)

Peaches—Mar 26–Apr 23
Pears—Mar 31–May 3
Apples—Apr 10–May 6
Harvest Range
Cherries—June 11–July 7
Apricots—June 27–July 22 (early) and June 28–July 18 (regular)
Peaches—Aug 4–Sept 6
Pears—Aug 7–Sept 8
Apples—Sept 4–Oct 17

For an updated report on what is blooming or ready to be picked, call the visitor center (435-425-3791). Press 1 for information and then press 5 for orchard information.

Weather

There is no bad season to visit Capitol Reef. It does get cold (below zero on some winter nights) and it does snow in the park, but seeing the red rock country with a fresh coat of white is an altogether different beauty worth seeing in person at least once. Trails can get muddy and slippery, and some portions could be covered with ice in certain conditions.

Temperatures will climb into the low 90s in July, but most other months have tolerable highs and lows on each end of the spectrum. Many visitors avoid the extremes and plan their trip in the spring or fall when temperatures are ideal for hiking and camping.

Always keep an eye to the skies and check the weather if possible before heading out on a hike. Monsoon rains in July, August, and September can produce intense thunderstorms creating a serious risk of flash flooding. Heavy rain even outside of the park can cause flash flooding in the national park's slot canyons and wash out roads.

Many times, an approaching flash flood can be heard coming. Head to higher ground if a low, roaring sound is coming from up canyon. The first floodwaters may not seem dangerous, but in some slow canyons, the water can reach 15 feet at peak.

Park service officials point out the following areas as being the most likely to experience flash floods during storm events: Grand Wash, Capitol Gorge, Sulphur Creek, Pleasant Creek, and Hall's Creek, as well as the slot canyons on the eastern side of the park along the Notom Road.

The park recommends these simple precautions:

- Observe weather conditions and use common sense.
- Do not enter a wash if a storm is threatening.
- If the wash begins to flow, climb to high ground. If in a vehicle, drive to points of ground on the road.
- If it is raining hard, but the wash is not flowing, begin to hike out or drive out on the road.
- Do not camp in wash bottoms.
- Remain on high ground until the water recedes.

Daily weather conditions and any closures due to weather are listed at the visitor center.

Rules and Regulations

The rules in Capitol Reef National Park are pretty self-explanatory, but it is always a good idea to read them so there are no surprises.

- Leave plants and animals, and their parts, along with fossils, minerals, and archaeological resources in their natural state.

It is against the law to possess, destroy, injure, deface, remove, dig, or disturb any item from its natural state.

- Carrying or possessing firearms in park facilities is prohibited. Carrying firearms must be in compliance with State of Utah law.
- View wildlife from a safe distance. Feeding, touching, teasing, frightening, or intentionally disturbing wildlife is prohibited. The use of wildlife calls and spotlights to view wildlife is not allowed.
- Pets must be kept under physical restraint and leashes may be no longer than 6 feet in length. Pets may not be left unattended while tied to an object. Pets are not allowed on park trails—although they are allowed on the trail between the visitor center and the campground or outside the road corridor.
- Fires are only allowed in designated camping and picnic areas with fire grates or portable fire pans capable of containing all ash and residue.
- Vehicles must remain on established roads or pullouts. Parked vehicles cannot obstruct roads.
- All roads are closed to the use of off-highway vehicles. This includes ATVs, OHVs, Razers, and dune buggies (whether street legal or not).
- The speed limit for the Scenic Driver is 25 mph, except through the picnic area/campground area, where it is 15 mph. The speed limit for Capitol Gorge, Grand Wash, and Pleasant Creek Road is 15 mph. The speed limit for the campground is 5 mph and for Hwy. 24 is 45 mph from the visitor center to the east boundary and 55 mph from the visitor center to the west boundary.

- Bicycles are prohibited off road or on any park trails except the trail between the visitor center and the campground.

- Horses and pack animals are allowed in most places in the park. Check with the park for closed areas and special regulations. Overnight trips require a backcountry permit.

- Camping is by permit with the exception of the Cedar Mesa and Cathedral campgrounds. Check at the visitor center or campground for specific regulations.

- The Fremont River waterfall is closed seasonally during the warm months. Alcohol, glass containers, and pets are prohibited at the Fremont River Waterfall year-round.

- Rock climbing is allowed with the exception of on any natural arch or bridge, within 300 feet of any archaeological site, or within ¼ mile of any nesting eagle, hawk, owl, or falcon. The placement of any new bolts or fixed hardware is prohibited.

- Fruit may be gathered and consumed free of charge in the orchards. A fee is charged when fruit is removed from the orchards. Tree climbing is prohibited in the orchards. Commercial resale is prohibited without a permit.

Safety and Preparation

Capitol Reef National Park is located in desert country. Water is a rarity, but when it comes, it can be lethal in the form of flash floods. Be prepared for both instances. Intense and dry heat can quickly lead to dehydration. Even if it is just to look at the petroglyphs along the boardwalk, carry a water bottle. Officials suggest a minimum of one gallon a day per person. People working actively in the sun, like hikers and backpackers, will need more. Temperatures in Capitol Reef peak around 100 degrees Fahrenheit during the summer months.

Wear the appropriate clothing to combat the heat (long-sleeved but light-weight shirt and shorts or pants), sunhat, and sunglasses. Flip-flops and sandals are not appropriate footwear for even the shortest of hikes. Stubbed toes, scratches, and bites on feet can ruin the rest of a vacation.

Do not count on your cell phone to provide a possible rescue. Cell phone coverage is sparse in the park.

Wildlife

Capitol Reef National Park is home to a surprisingly wide range of wildlife, ranging from venomous snakes to rare birds to bighorn sheep and even mountain lions. Respect all wildlife by leaving it alone. Here is a look at some of the wildlife visitors to the park might encounter and how to act if you do.

Visitors in the park will notice plenty of mule deer. The deer native to the West are particularly common in the orchards where they find easy food. Many people consider deer to be tame and approach them for pictures. But they are wild animals and pack a serious kick if they feel threatened. Keep your distance and help protect deer by not feeding them human food.

Mother deer with young fawns can be aggressive if they sense danger, so avoid getting close. Buck mule deer with large antlers can be dangerous in the fall when it is mating season. Keep a safe distance if you come across bucks or groups of those at that time of year.

Mountain lions focus on high concentrations of deer, like those that gather near the orchards. Carcasses of deer killed by mountain lions have been found near and in the orchards. Pay attention when in Capitol Reef, and avoid hiking alone. If you draw the attention of a mountain lion, do not run. Walk backward toward safety. If the lion continues to approach, wave your arms and legs to try and appear larger. If the cat continues to be aggressive, throw rocks and branches at it while yelling and hope it realizes you are not something it should spend its energy on. If you spot a mountain lion in Capitol Reef, report it to a ranger.

Other predators in the park include coyotes and gray foxes. There is a chance you will see coyotes, but you will be lucky to spot either of these canines in the park.

Desert bighorn sheep were eradicated from the Capitol Reef National Park area due to over hunting and the introduction of disease from domestic sheep. For years, the only bighorn sheep to be spotted in the park were the numerous petroglyphs featuring the native mammals of southern Utah. In 1996, the National Park Service conducted a trapping operation in Canyonlands National Park, also in Utah, and brought twenty bighorn sheep to Capitol Reef. That number was augmented in 1997 with another twenty animals and today there is a naturally sustained population of bighorn sheep in the park. Bighorn are not a common sight in Capitol Reef, but their growing numbers will increase the chances of visitors spotting them.

While there is one venomous snake found in the park, the midget faded rattlesnake is usually not aggressive and few hikers will encounter one on the trail. If you do, give the snake plenty of room and everyone should be fine to go on their way. The Great Basin gopher snake is often mistaken for the midget faded rattlesnake. The mistaken identity is often due to the gopher snake mimicking a rattlesnake in an attempt to protect itself by hissing and trying to vibrate its tail. The gopher snake is not dangerous to people. Rattlesnakes have triangular heads and there is no mistaking the sound of real rattles. Midget faded rattlesnakes will only reach a length of about 24 inches. Gopher snakes, on the other hand, can grow longer than 100 inches—that is more than 8 feet!

The desert side-blotched lizard can often be spotted sunning itself on rocks around the park and even near the campground. The side-blotched lizard is recognized due to a bluish blotch on each side behind its front legs. Other species of lizards common in the park include the eastern fence lizard and western or Great Basin whiptail.

Among the small mammals of Capitol Reef, rabbit is one people enjoy spotting and one they make sure to stay away from. Desert cottontail rabbits and black-tailed jackrabbits can both be observed in the park. Jackrabbits are usually running when spotted, while cottontails prefer to lay low when they feel threatened.

Skunks do not typically present a problem for hikers. Just give them a wide berth and leave them alone. Campers, on the other hand, may sometimes get a visit from this odorous creature. Skunks are nocturnal and will often tour the campground at night looking for scraps left out by messy campers. Avoid an encounter with a skunk by cleaning up before climbing into the tent.

Bats are also a common sighting when the sun goes down. They are most visible at dusk, when they emerge to feast on the insects that frequent the area around the Fremont River.

More than 230 species of birds have been identified at Capitol Reef National Park, many of them found along the

Fremont River. Raptors including peregrine falcons, golden eagles, and even Mexican spotted owls (listed as threatened on the Endangered Species List) can be found in the park.

Observant listeners will often hear the distinct call of the canyon wren echoing in the red rock canyons of Capitol Reef National Park.

Common feathered friends at the park include ravens and chukars.

Follow these rules regarding wildlife for your safety and the well-being of the animals.

- Do not attempt to pet or touch any animals.
- Stay at least 30 feet from deer.
- Do not feed wild animals.
- Keep pets on a leash at all times.
- Leave a fawn mule deer found lying on the ground alone. Fawns often bed down while their mothers continue to feed. Once a human touches a fawn, it is possible the mother will abandon it.
- Do not jog or hike alone, particularly at dusk and dawn.
- Keep children close. Do not allow unsupervised children to play along riverbanks or in heavy vegetation, particularly at dusk and dawn.
- If you spot a mountain lion you feel is being aggressive, wave your arms, shout, and throw rocks at the animal. If children are with you, pick them up. Do not attempt to hide or crouch. Hold your ground or back away slowly. Do not turn your back on a mountain lion. If attacked, fight back and try to keep the animal in front of you.
- Report all mountain lion sightings to a ranger or at the visitor center.

Plants

The varied terrain and ecological niches of Capitol Reef National Park leads to a wide variety of plants, some of them unique to the park. Among the 887 plant species identified in the park are more than forty rare and endemic species, of which six are federally listed as threatened or endangered.

The Fremont cottonwood tree is a favorite among visitors. The large leafy trees can be found lining the entire stretch of the Fremont River as it runs through the park and anywhere in the park with a semi-reliable source of water. The trees provide a great green contrast to the red rock country of the desert park in the spring and summer. It is, however, in the fall when the cottonwoods become a target for the photographers. Utah has its share of amazing fall destinations, but Capitol Reef is one of the best as the cottonwood leaves turn yellow before falling to the desert floor.

The pinyon pine is found at slightly higher altitudes in the park and is the second largest plant in the park. This pine tree produces large seeds, also known as pine nuts, which are very popular food items for both animals and people.

The other common large plant in the park is the Utah juniper. Often mistakenly called a cedar tree, the juniper is a common sight in many large open areas of the park. Junipers provide an important food resource for a variety of wildlife species.

Cacti are also found in Capitol Reef National Park. One of our favorites is the fishhook cactus. This small cactus of the barrel variety has yellow or pink flowers that bloom in May and June. The claret cup cactus is often found in bunches and displays red flowers in the spring and summer.

Sagebrush, an important part of the desert ecosystem, is a common sight in some portions of the park. Rain may not be something hikers want to experience in Capitol Reef because it can lead to flash flooding and muddy trails, but the smell of wet sagebrush is arguably one of the most enjoyable and relaxing scents in the world.

Globemallow, paintbrush, primrose, sego lilies, and phlox all add to the colorscape of the desert environment in the park.

It is illegal to pick and remove plants from Capitol Reef. Enjoy the plants and flowers in the park with pictures, but leave them on the ground. Tell children why it is important to leave the plants so others can enjoy them while wandering the trails of the park. You might also consider warning them about cactus needles. It seems like in every third or fourth trip, somebody in our group finds a way to get cactus needles stuck in their hands while climbing on rocks or in their feet while wearing sandals.

Night sky?

Capitol Reef has become the seventh unit of the National Park Service to achieve designation as an International Dark Sky Park by the International Dark-Sky Association. The designation of Capitol Reef National Park as a "Gold Tier" park, signifying the highest quality night skies, comes during International Dark Sky Week, an annual event to raise awareness of light pollution and celebrate the beauty of the night sky.

Geology

The national park part of Capitol Reef National Park has only been around since 1971 (it was originally named a monument in 1937), but the land around the park has been around for much longer.

Scientists report approximately 10,000 feet of sedimentary strata—layers of rock for us laymen—is found in, and around, Capitol Reef. The rocks have been aged from the Cretaceous Period (about 80 million years old) to material from the Permian Period (about 270 million years ago).

The youngest rocks are found on the eastern edge of Capitol Reef and the oldest on the western half of the national park.

Capitol Dome, one of the park's most recognized features and so named because it looks similar to the building in Washington, D.C., is comprised of Navajo Sandstone from the Jurassic Period.

The different layers of strata were formed when the land where the park is now saw various and very different environments. At different times through the years, Capitol Reef was under a shallow ocean, was a vast desert of moving sand, and was a tropical forest with swamps and rivers. It is hard to imagine any of those scenarios while hiking through the park.

Parts of Capitol Reef are dominated by certain time frames and the corresponding rock formations. The massive monoliths of the Cathedral Valley in the northern portion of the park are comprised of a reddish-orange Entrada Sandstone formed 140–180 million years ago. They have eroded in quite a different way than, say, Capitol Dome.

The harder sandstone layers, like the Wingate and Navajo, typically form cliffs as a result of erosion. Soft layers, like the Chinle Formation from the Triassic Period, erode easily into hill and slopes. Those slopes are typically void of vegetation because they include bentonitic clays, which are not a favorable growing environment for plants.

Geologists believe most of the erosion we see today only really got going about twenty million years ago when the Colorado Plateau underwent some major uplift.

Other geologic wonders of interest include the black boulders found in the Fremont River Valley. Geologists say these black rocks showed up twenty to thirty million years ago from lava flows on nearby Boulder and Thousand Lake mountains. The boulders carried to Capitol Reef at the end of the Ice Age as landslides, debris flows, and massive stream surges from melting glaciers made serious changes to the landscape.

Even if you are not a geology geek, most visitors to Capitol Reef National Park can appreciate the amazing geology that makes the place so uniquely beautiful.

Resource Protection

The desert environment of southern Utah is extreme, but it is also surprisingly fragile. Stay on trails while hiking in the park. The soil is alive in certain spots, and it has taken decades to become established. Avoid taking shortcuts and follow all the principles of Leave No Trace ethics.

Visitor Information

Information about hiking in Capitol Reef National Park can be found at the visitor center. Details about hiking, backpacking and camping in the park can also be found on the web at www.nps.gov/care.

How to Use This Guide

Each region begins with a section introduction, where you are given a sweeping look at the lay of the land. After this general overview, specific hikes within that region are described. You will learn about the terrain and what surprises each route has to offer.

This guide is designed to be simple and easy to use. Each hike is described with a map and summary information that delivers the trail's vital statistics including length, difficulty, fees and permits, park hours, canine compatibility, and trail contacts. Directions to the trailhead are also provided, along with a general description of what you will see along the way.

How the Hikes Were Chosen

This guide describes trails that are accessible to almost every hiker ranging in length from 0.1 of a mile to more than 5 miles. Hikes range in difficulty from flat excursions perfect for a family outing to more challenging treks for more experienced hikers.

Selecting a Hike

Trail difficulty is a subjective matter. The National Park Service has provided these ratings and descriptions. The park service, like most federal agencies, tends to rate hikes a little more difficult than they typically are, so visitors feel like they have completed a more challenging hike rather than say the journey was much more difficult than they expected.

Easy hikes are typically short and mostly flat, taking anywhere from 20 to 90 minutes to complete.

Moderate hikes involve increased distance and relatively mild changes in elevation and may take 1–2 hours to complete.

Strenuous hikes feature some steep stretches, greater distances, and generally take longer than 2 hours to complete.

Trail Finder

Best Hikes to Arches and Natural Bridges

Best Water Hikes

Best Hikes with Children

Best Hikes with Slot Canyons

Best Sunset Hikes

Best Panoramic Views

Best Remote Hikes

Map Legend

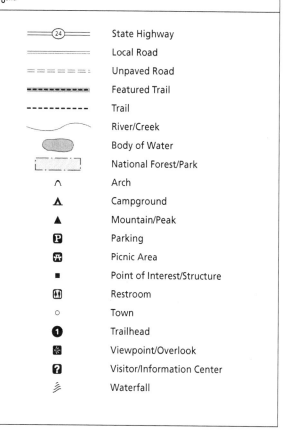

	State Highway
	Local Road
	Unpaved Road
	Featured Trail
	Trail
	River/Creek
	Body of Water
	National Forest/Park
∩	Arch
▲	Campground
▲	Mountain/Peak
🅿	Parking
⛩	Picnic Area
■	Point of Interest/Structure
🚻	Restroom
○	Town
❶	Trailhead
	Viewpoint/Overlook
❓	Visitor/Information Center
≷	Waterfall

Fruita Historic District

The majority of hikes in this guide are located in the Fruita Historic District and Scenic Drive area of Capitol Reef National Park. As visitors might expect, this is the busiest part of the park and hikers are likely to see others on the trails. The Fruita Campground is arguably one of the most scenic and unique in the National Park System. Surrounded by orchards, the campground is predominately grass and includes a large tent-only area. This is a good place for families as the area provides things outside of hiking if the family is tuckered out from chasing lizards and climbing cool rock formations.

The Capitol Reef National Park Visitor Center is located on Hwy. 24 eight miles east of the town of Torrey. The visitor center is in the Fruita District and serves as the heart of the park. Visitors can find detailed weather forecasts—particularly important when planning hikes in areas that experience flash floods—or pick up a free backcountry permit (required for all overnight trips). National Park Service staffers and volunteers are on hand to answer questions about the park. Visitors can also find schedules and topics for ranger programs and pick up Junior Ranger workbooks. The visitor center is open from 8 a.m. to 4:30 p.m. but has varied extended hours during the peak seasons (spring through fall). The Capitol Reef Natural History Association provides books, shirts, pictures, and other items for purchase at the visitor center. A movie on the park is shown for those with time. Restrooms and water are also available.

Ripple Rock Nature Center is south of Hwy. 24 on the Scenic Drive. The nature center is typically open from Memorial Day to Labor Day—check at the visitor center for days and hours the center is open. Families can participate in a variety of traditional pioneer activities and learn about the park's geology, wildlife, and plants.

The historic Gifford House store and museum typically opens each year on March 14 (Pi Day) and closes on October 31. The Gifford House is a great place to pick up baked goodies for the trail or enjoy homemade pies and cinnamon rolls after a day exploring the park. Local craft goods are also available for purchase. The Gifford House is open daily from 8 a.m. to 5 p.m. with extended hours during the summer months.

The Scenic Drive, which provides access to multiple trailheads in Capitol Reef, starts at the visitor center and heads south, providing access to the Ripple Rock Nature Center, the historic Gifford House, Fruita Campground, the Fruita Amphitheater, Capitol Gorge, and Grand Wash. There is a fee required to drive the Scenic Road past the Fruita Campground at a self-pay station.

It is hard not to fall into the cliché of referring to the Fruita Campground as an oasis. Water from the Fremont River provides a lush and green setting compared to the arid desert and red rock environment surrounding it. Fruit trees frame the campground and provide fresh treats at various times throughout the season. There are sixty-four recreational vehicle/tent sites on three loops in the Fruita Campground. There are also seven walk-in tent sites, which are unfortunately placed next to the sometime busy Scenic Drive. Each site has a picnic table and firepit. There is no water, sewage, or electrical hookups. An RV dump and potable water fill station is situated near the entrance to the A and B loops. The entire campground is available on a first-come, first-serve basis. No reservations are possible, and there is no "saving" a site for people on their way. Restrooms are scattered round the campground. There are no showers.

A large and private group site is also available and it can be reserved on www.recreation.gov. The group site is typically available from April 1 to October 24 each year but is closed on Tuesday and Wednesday nights for maintenance.

Less than a mile east of the visitor center on Hwy. 24 is the Historic Fruita Schoolhouse. The one-room schoolhouse was opened in 1896 after a local fourteen-year-old was teaching in a backyard for years. Students in grades 1 through 8 attended the school at the same time. Classes ranged from eight to twenty-six students. As one of the best-constructed buildings in town, the schoolhouse also served as the church, town hall, and dance hall. The school was closed in 1941 as the population of Fruita continued to shrink. The schoolhouse is not open except during special ranger tours typically held each day during the summer. Check at the visitor center for a schedule of the tours. Visitors are welcome to stop at the schoolhouse and peer through the windows. The classroom is set up as it would have been when the last students attended the school. The Fruita Schoolhouse was placed on the National Register of Historic Places in 1964. The park service restored the structure to match the 1930s.

It is easy to see the art of the ancient people who lived in the region at the easily accessible petroglyph panels just over a mile east of the visitor center on Hwy. 24. The panels, believed created from AD 600 to 1330, were a part of the Fremont culture. Boardwalks and viewing scopes help visitors get an up-close look at the rock art, leaving many wondering exactly what the images might mean.

1 Capitol Gorge and the Tanks

Start: Trailhead located at the end of the Scenic Drive in Capitol Gorge

Distance: 2 miles out-and-back

Hiking time: 1–2 hours

Difficulty: Easy, with a short but steep hike to the Tanks

Trail surface: Canyon floor, some sand, slickrock

Best season: Year-round

Other trail users: Golden Throne

Fees and permits: An entrance fee is required to drive the Scenic Drive past the Fruita Campground.

The permit, which is available for a fee for individuals (bicycles or pedestrians) and a slightly higher fee for vehicles, is good for 7 days

Maps: Park map and brochure available at the visitor center

Trail contact: Capitol Reef National Park, HC 70, Box 15, Torrey, Utah, 84775; www.nps. gov/care

Finding the trailhead: Head south from the visitor center on the Scenic Drive for 7.8 miles where the road turns into a graded dirt road entering Capitol Gorge. The trailhead is 2.2 miles down the Gorge

The Hike

Capitol Gorge once served as a road through the rough desert country of southern Utah. It became unnecessary in 1962 when Hwy. 24 was completed. Visitors to Capitol Reef still drive down a portion of Capitol Gorge, but only to the trailhead. Flash floods can hit this road hard, so pay special attention to the weather forecast and avoid visiting if storms are threatening. If you doubt the power of a flash flood, consider that vehicles left in the parking areas or abandoned along the road in Capitol Gorge and Grand Wash when rain hits are often carried down the canyon and deposited upside down. Visitors who ignored flash flood warnings are often stranded when caught in high water.

The old road makes for easy walking, and after a few minutes, hikers come to a petroglyph panel created by the Fremont people. More recent visitors to the Gorge left their signatures on the wall a little further down the path on the opposite side of the canyon on the south wall. These six signatures are from members of a US Geological Survey team in 1911.

That is just the tip of the iceberg of signatures in Capitol Gorge. Next along the hike is the Pioneer Register. The earliest signatures from two pioneers is dated 1871. Others followed down the years, as the Gorge was a major route through canyon country. While rock art and the Pioneer Register are considered historic, it is important to note that defacing canyons walls in today's world is illegal. Remind people if you see them trying to add their signature or art and then report them.

After hiking 0.8 of a mile, visitors will come to a sign for The Tanks. Tanks, also commonly referred to as potholes in desert terminology, refer to pockets where water holds in pools carved by erosion in the sandstone. In many years of visiting, I only came across the tanks void of water once. It was late in the year and it had been a dry summer. The kids loved playing in the soft, cool sand of the Tanks that year. We remarked on what a wonderful sandbox the Tanks made for the kids. The Tanks are accessed by a steep 0.2-mile trail. Scour the area around the potholes and look for a small natural bridge. When water is in the tanks, carefully study the pool and you may likely see tadpoles and aquatic insects taking advantage of the oasis in the desert.

Keep your eyes out for desert bighorn sheep and not just those on the rock art in the Gorge. The animals disappeared from this country due to uncontrolled hunting and disease. I was lucky enough to be part of a National Park Service effort in the mid-1990s to capture forty desert bighorn at Canyonlands National Park and relocate them to Capitol Reef. Some fifteen years later, my family spotted a herd of bighorn as we walked up the Tanks. It was a wonderful moment to realize I was seeing the impact of that bighorn relocation effort.

Most people turn around after visiting the Tanks and make the 1-mile journey back to the parking area. Some visitors continue along Capitol Gorge to the park boundary. In his book *Capitol Reef National Park: The Complete Hiking and Touring Guide*, Stinchfield writes walking to the boundary and back to the trailhead adds 3.2 miles to the trip.

Miles and Directions

0.0	From the trailhead hike east in Capitol Gorge.
0.125	Look for Fremont petroglyphs on the left. After another 100 yards, look high on the well for the signatures of the USGS team from 1911 on the south side of the canyon.
0.75	The first signatures of the Pioneer Register.
0.80	Look for a sign to The Tanks on the north side of the Gorge (0.2 mile from the canyon floor to The Tanks).
1.0	The Tanks.
2.0	Arrive back at the trailhead.

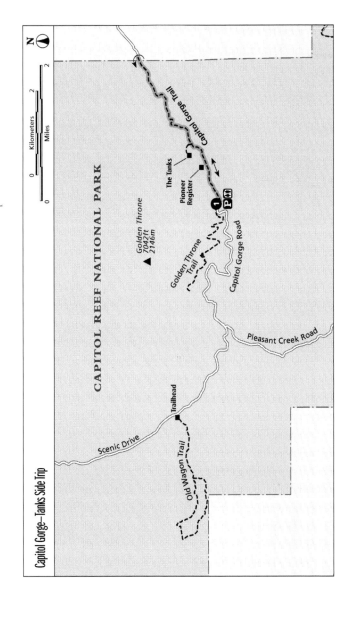

Capitol Gorge–Tanks Side Trip

CAPITOL REEF NATIONAL PARK

N

Kilometers
0   1   2

Miles
0   1   2

Golden Throne
7042 ft
2146 m

The Tanks

Pioneer Register

Capitol Gorge Trail

Golden Throne Trail

Capitol Gorge Road

Pleasant Creek Road

Scenic Drive

Trailhead

Old Wagon Trail

P ♿
1

2 Grand Wash

Start: The Grand Wash Trailhead or on the other end of the canyon on Hwy. 24
Distance: 2.5 miles one-way or 5 miles round-trip
Hiking time: 2–3 hours
Difficulty: Easy
Trail surface: Rock and sand
Other trail users: Cassidy Arch Trail; Frying Pan Trail
Best season: Year-round
Fees and permits: An entrance fee is required to drive the Scenic Drive past the Fruita Campground.
The permit, which is available for a fee for individuals (bicycles or pedestrians) and a slightly higher fee for vehicles, is good for 7 days
Maps: Park map and brochure available at the visitor center
Trail contact: Capitol Reef National Park, HC 70, Box 15, Torrey, Utah, 84775; www.nps.gov/care

Finding the trailhead: Take the Scenic Road to the Grand Wash dirt road. The trailhead is 1.25 miles after the turn. If hiking from Hwy. 24, look for the pullout on the right 4.5 miles east of the visitor center just past the Hickman Bridge parking lot

The Hike

This is a flat hike with mostly firm ground, which makes it popular with easily intimidated visitors. Do not expect much alone time. On busy summer days, you will rarely go a few minutes without seeing other hikers. Some people get dropped off on one end of the Gorge and have a ride waiting for them on the other end, but most people just wander the Gorge as long as they like and then turn around. My family typically walks in from the west side via the Scenic Drive and turns around when the scenery starts to feel repetitive. The good thing about hiking the deep canyons of Capitol Reef is the ability to find shade on hot days. Grand Wash is an option if you are limited to hiking in the middle of the day during the hottest part of the year.

Unlike Capitol Gorge, there are not a lot of historic signatures, rock art of tanks to see on this hike. Like Capitol Gorge, this canyon can be dangerous during flash floods. Check in at the visitor center for a weather report before starting the hike. Remember, rain miles away can trigger flash floods where you plan to hike.

The most striking detail of the Grand Wash hike for most people starts about a mile in when the canyon narrows to about 16 feet wide. The walls at this point are roughly 600 feet high according to park officials. Staring up to the top makes some visitors dizzy.

Grand Wash is a good choice when the park is busy and Capitol Gorge is crowded.

Miles and Directions

0.0 Head east from the parking area in Grand Wash.

0.75 A trailmarker for Cassidy Arch is on the left. This connects to the Frying Pan Trail, which links to the Cohab Canyon trail which leads back to the Fruita Campground near the Gifford House.

1.0 The Narrows.

2.5 Hwy. 24.

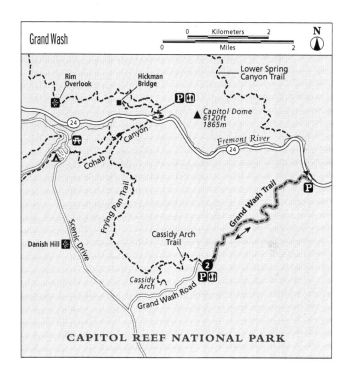

3 Cohab Canyon

Start: Scenic Drive near the Fruita Campground across from the photogenic Pendleton Barn near the Fruita Campground or from Hwy. 24

Distance: 1.7 miles or 2.8 miles with viewpoints

Hiking time: 2–3 hours

Difficulty: Moderate, steep for first 0.25 mile and then easy

Trail surface: Packed-dirt, slick-rock, and sand

Other trail users: Cassidy Arch Trail; Frying Pan Trail

Best season: Year-round

Fees and permits: No fee required

Maps: Park map and brochure available at the visitor center

Trail contact: Capitol Reef National Park, HC 70, Box 15, Torrey, Utah, 84775; www.nps.gov/care

Finding the trailhead: Cohab starts from the Scenic Drive near the Fruita Campground across from the Pendleton Barn or from Hwy. 24 across from the Hickman Bridge parking lot

The Hike

This has become a traditional first hike of the trip for my family when we are staying in the Fruita Campground. It is a good one for kids if you can get them past the first steep portion. Stop and let them rest in the first ¼ mile. As you turn around, take great pictures of the barn, homestead, and campground from the higher ground. We enjoy stopping at the top where the canyon starts and waving back to family or friends who stayed behind to make dinner and set up camp. Make sure people in the camp have a camera ready to take pictures of the hikers and vice versa.

Once in the canyon, children and adults alike quickly become smitten with narrow slots to sneak into and the crazy "hole canyon" formations—sometimes called honeycombs. Many a picture has been taken with kids peering through red rock holes in Cohab Canyon. Kids on our hikes enjoy sitting down on the trail in the sandy areas and just running the fine red sand through their toes and fingers. We all agree Capitol Reef sand is the best camping sand in the world—followed closely by the sand near the Devils Garden campground in Arches National Park. A surprising variety of plants can be found in the canyon and in Capitol Reed as a whole. We enjoy seeing common paintbrush tucked in "secret" places along the trail. Take only pictures and leave the plants alone. Discourage youngsters from picking flowers for mom by telling them that once removed some plants will not return.

Just over a mile from the campground, hikers will come to a sign indicating the Fruita Overlook trail. This trail leads to two overlooks and will add about 1.2 miles to the hike. If you have time to add the extra distance, it is worth the effort to take in the views.

Soon after the Overlook Trail, hikers will see the junction with the Frying Pan Trail. Those looking for a longer adventure might consider getting dropped off in Grand Wash at the trailhead and hiking the Cassidy Arch Trail and then joining the Frying Pan Trail which connects with Cohab Canyon. If you take time to visit the viewpoints, hikers will have covered about 8.2 miles when back at the campground.

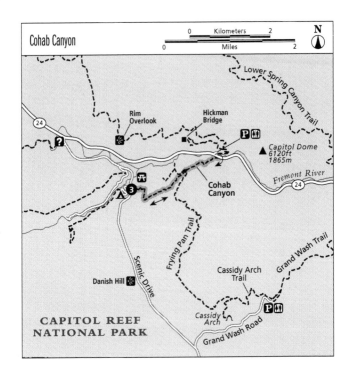

Cohab Canyon

0   Kilometers   2

0   Miles   2

N

Lower Spring Canyon Trail

Rim Overlook

Hickman Bridge

Capitol Dome
6120ft
1865m

Cohab Canyon

Fremont River

Frying Pan Trail

Cassidy Arch Trail

Grand Wash Trail

Danish Hill

Scenic Drive

CAPITOL REEF
NATIONAL PARK

Cassidy Arch

Grand Wash Road

Miles and Directions

0.0   Start from the Scenic Drive just across from the Pendleton Barn.

0.25 Enter the canyon.

1.0   Junctions with the Fruita Overlook and Frying Pan trails.

1.7   Hwy. 24 at Hickman Bridge.

4 Golden Throne

Start: End of the Capitol Gorge Road

Distance: 4 miles out-and-back

Hiking time: 2–3 hours

Difficulty: Strenuous

Trail surface: Slickrock, packed dirt

Other trail users: Capitol Gorge

Best season: Year-round

Fees and permits: An entrance fee is required to take the Scenic Drive past the Fruita Campground. The permit, which is available for a fee for individuals (bicycles or pedestrians) and a slightly higher fee for vehicles, is good for 7 days

Maps: Park map and brochure available at the visitor center

Trail contact: Capitol Reef National Park, HC 70, Box 15, Torrey, Utah, 84775; www.nps.gov/care

Finding the trailhead: Head south from the visitor center on the Scenic Drive for 7.8 miles where the road turns into graded dirt entering Capitol Gorge. The trailhead is 2.2 miles down the gorge. A sign for the actual start of the trail is visible from the parking lot on the north side of the canyon

The Hike

The trail is a series of somewhat steep climbs followed by flat stretches for the length of the hike. There are a couple of exposed cliff edges, but most people seem to have no issue with the trail. A first glimpse of Golden Throne comes just when stepping onto a new flat.

Depending on the time of year, the flats can be a good place to look at the diverse plant life found in Capitol Reef. Hikers will find everything from cactus to Mormon tea to juniper.

Just before the end of the trail, a small natural amphitheater does a wonderful job of echoing voices. Give it a try before hitting the trail again.

The hike ends at a very helpful sign "Trail's End." Steep cliffs at the base of Golden Throne, more of a brownish-reddish-white color actually, do prevent getting any closer to the massive formation. From the end of the trail, you can also spot the Henry Mountains to the east. Many hikers plan their trip for the late afternoon in hopes they will catch the Throne as golden as it gets in the setting sun. It is then the landmark turns golden.

If you did not get enough of Golden Throne from the hike, there are plenty of other places in the park to catch a glimpse of the formation. One of the most popular is a viewpoint on the Capitol Gorge Road about 0.7 of a mile from the trailhead.

Miles and Directions

0.0   Start at the Capitol Gorge Trailhead. Look to the north for the sign for Golden Throne.

2.0   Arrive at the sign "Trail's End" and a spectacular view of Golden Throne.

4.0   Arrive back at the trailhead.

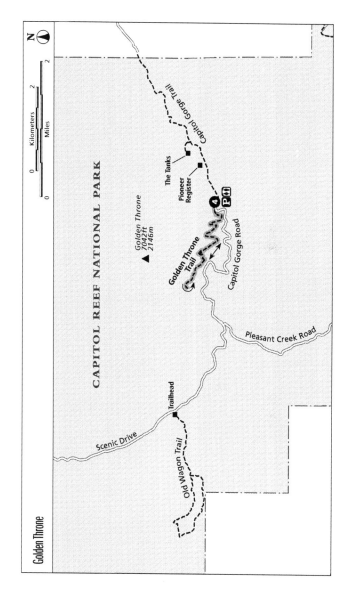

Golden Throne

5 Old Wagon Trail

Start: 6.5 miles south of the visitor center on the Scenic Drive to a pullout
Distance: 3.75 miles
Hiking time: 2-3 hours
Difficulty: Strenuous
Trail surface: Packed dirt, rocks
Best season: Spring, winter, and fall
Fees and permits: An entrance fee is required to drive the Scenic Drive past the Fruita Campground.

The permit, which is available for a fee for individuals (bicycles or pedestrians) and a slightly higher fee for vehicles, is good for 7 days
Maps: Park map and brochure available at the visitor center
Trail contact: Capitol Reef National Park, HC 70, Box 15, Torrey, Utah, 84775; www.nps. gov/care

Finding the trailhead: Look for a pullout 6.5 miles south of the visitor center on the Scenic Drive. It will be on the right and there is a sign indicating the start of the hike. The pullout will hold up to four cars

The Hike

If you start to feel a little claustrophobic while doing the hikes in Capitol Gorge and Grand Wash, the Old Wagon Trail might be what you are looking for as an escape. The open country on the west side of the Scenic Drive is a contrast to the red rock canyons on the east side of the valley. Pinyon pine and juniper trees provide some green along the trail.

Because it lacks the geologic features of other Capitol Reef trails, the Old Wagon Trail is a good choice if you are looking for alone time in the desert while in the Fruita District.

As its name mentions, the draw in this hike is walking along part of an old trail used by pioneers crossing the desert in wagons. The road was a shortcut between the town of Grover to the west on Hwy. 12 and Capitol Gorge.

There is quite an elevation gain in the hike—1,100 feet in the first 1.7 miles. Visitors should avoid the Old Wagon Trail on hot days. This might be a good option if you do not mind getting a little wet when rain closes other trails due to flash flood threats.

The loop portion starts just over a mile into the journey. Park officials suggest hikers take the loop to the left. Once you start the loop, you are on the Old Wagon Trail. After 2.4 miles, hikers will see a sign for a viewpoint just off the loop. Landmarks visible from the lookout include the Henry Mountains, the mouth of Capitol Gorge, Golden Throne, the Thousand Lake Mountains, Chimney Rock, Grand Wash, and Ferns Nipple.

Walk back to the loop and rejoin the trail back to the Scenic Drive knowing it is all downhill.

Miles and Directions

0.0 Begin hiking north on the trail just west of the parking area.

0.50 Two sets of steps.

1.0 Loop portion of the trail—head clockwise.

2.4 Spur trail to viewpoint.

3.75 Arrive back at the pullout.

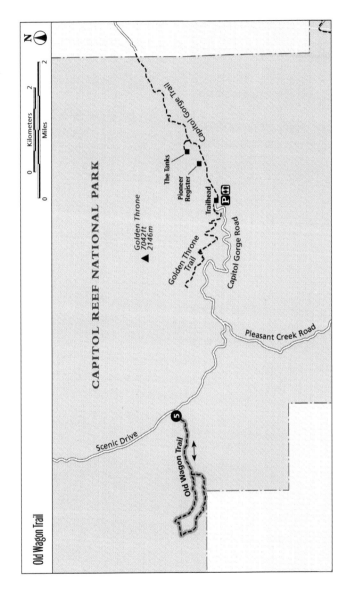

Old Wagon Trail

CAPITOL REEF NATIONAL PARK

Golden Throne
7042ft
2146m

The Tanks

Pioneer
Register

Trailhead

Capitol Gorge Trail

Golden Throne
Trail

Capitol Gorge Road

Pleasant Creek Road

Scenic Drive

5

Old Wagon Trail

N

Kilometers

Miles

0   2

0   2

6 Hickman Bridge

Start: Hickman Bridge parking area and trailhead on Hwy. 24
Distance: 2.0 miles
Hiking time: 1.5-2 hours
Difficulty: Moderate
Trail surface: Slickrock and packed dirt
Best season: Year-round
Other trail users: Rim Overlook, Navajo Knobs

Fees and permits: No fees or permits required
Maps: Park map and brochure available at the visitor center
Trail contact: Capitol Reef National Park, HC 70, Box 15, Torrey, Utah, 84775; www.nps.gov/care

Finding the trailhead: The Hickman Bridge parking area and trailhead is 1.9 miles east of the visitor center on Hwy. 24

The Hike

Hickman Bridge is the must-see formation at Capitol Reef National Park. Naturally, this is one of the most popular hikes in the park. The natural land bridge is 133 feet long and 125 feet off the ground at the highest point. It was named after Utah Legislator Joseph S. Hickman, who worked to have the area created as a national monument.

There is a trail guide available on a post near the start of the trail with a small voluntary donation. The guide is worth it, particularly for first-time users of the trail.

The first portion of the trail can be intimidating as it climbs away from the Fremont River, but after the steep ascent, hikers reach a short flat with scattered islands of vegetation. After 0.30 of a mile, there is a sign pointing to the right for the Rim Overlook and Navajo Knobs. Turn left and head for Hickman Bridge.

After the flat, the trail climbs a little more and then drops into a sandy wash. Look for a granary believed to be built by people from the Fremont culture in an alcove on a cliff to the north. It can be hard to spot in some light conditions and easier in others.

Just a stone's throw away up the wash is a popular stop for family scrapbook photos. Two natural bridges have been formed in slickrock at the top of the wash. My family calls one "Sand Hole." People like to stand above or below the hole and take pictures through the opening. It is a fun snapshot framing the photo either way.

The trail to Hickman Bridge continues out of the wash just before the small bridges. Hickman first comes into view while climbing out of the wash.

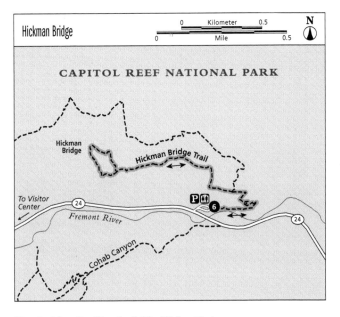

A few more minutes of hiking will get visitors to a short loop trail to the "back" side of the bridge. Most people continue up the same wash and return to the main trail on the loop after visiting Hickman.

Soon after the break is a good place to stop and take a picture. Hickman Bridge is tough to photograph because it blends in with the cliffs behind. Test angles to help people see the distinction of the bridge in your photos. It is fun to watch as people try to figure out the best angle to capture Hickman in a picture. Many of the best pictures come from the west side of Hickman against the rock looking toward the trail.

The loop trail provides a nice view of the Fremont River and Fruita from a high point.

Because the sun rarely reaches under Hickman Bridge, many visitors take the opportunity to escape the sun, enjoy the wonder of the natural bridge, and have water and a snack.

Chances are high you will see other visitors on the trail. Consider visiting the park at "off times" to experience it on your own terms.

One of my favorite memories of hiking to Hickman Bridge came just after several inches of snow had fallen in February. It was, in fact, the only time out of dozens of trips that I did not see another soul on the trail. Those who have not been in red rock country with snow are missing out. The clash of colors is striking and vivid.

Miles and Directions

- **0.0** Start at the Hickman Bridge Trailhead on Hwy. 24.
- **0.3** Trail splits to Rim Overlook and Navajo Knobs Trail. Stay left.
- **1.0** Arrive under Hickman Bridge.
- **2.0** Arrive back at the trailhead.

7 Rim Overlook

Start: Hickman Bridge Trailhead
Distance: 4.4 miles round-trip
Hiking time: 4-5 hours
Difficulty: Strenuous
Trail surface: Packed dirt, slickrock
Best season: Spring and fall
Other trail users: Hickman Bridge, Navajo Knobs

Fees and permits: No permit required
Maps: Park map and brochure available at the visitor center
Trail contact: Capitol Reef National Park, HC 70, Box 15, Torrey, Utah, 84775; www.nps. gov/care

Finding the trailhead: The Hickman Bridge parking area and trailhead is 1.9 miles east of the visitor center on Hwy. 24

The Hike

Visitors looking for a little longer day hike from the Hickman Bridge Trailhead often head out for the Rim Overlook hike and throw in a side trip to the bridge for good measure. This side jaunt adds 1.6 miles to the Rim Overlook hike.

People without time to make the side trip will get a chance to see Hickman Bridge while on the Rim Overlook Trail. The trail climbs out of a wash and up switchbacks to a ridge. About five minutes later, a sign will appear indicating the way to the Hickman Bridge Overlook. As is the case with a first glimpse on the Hickman Bridge Trail, it can be hard to spot the natural bridge at first because it blends in with the surroundings. Hickman will, however, eventually reveal itself. Standing to the left of the sign seems to be the best vantage point.

A series of four flats await hikers for the next mile before hitting the "Rim Overlook" sign. The trail has climbed more than 1,100 feet in elevation at this point. Even if your legs

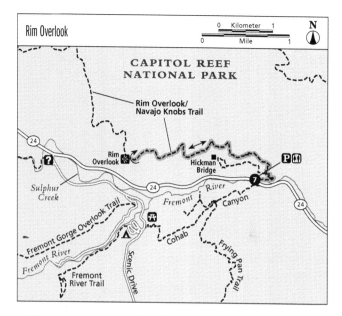

CAPITOL REEF
NATIONAL PARK

Rim Overlook/
Navajo Knobs Trail

Rim
Overlook

Hickman
Bridge

Sulphur
Creek

Fremont   River   Canyon

Fremont Gorge Overlook Trail

Cohab

Frying Pan Trail

Fremont River

Scenic Drive

Fremont
River Trail

and lungs do not appreciate the hike, your eyes certainly will. Can you spot the old schoolhouse just below? Trained eyes will be able to pick out the Abajo, Henry, and Boulder mountains in the distance from the viewpoint. Landmarks a little closer geographically include the Fruita Historic District and orchards, Ferns Nipple, and the entrance to Cohab Canyon.

If you are still feeling adventurous, the trail to Navajo Knobs is another 2 miles down the trail.

Miles and Directions

0.0 Start at the Hickman Bridge Trailhead on Hwy. 24.

0.3 Arrive at the junction to Hickman Bridge. Stay right for the Rim Overlook and Navajo Knobs destinations.

2.2 Sign for Rim Overlook marks the end of the hike.

4.4 Arrive back at the trailhead.

8 Goosenecks and Sunset Point

Start: Panorama Point parking area

Distance: 0.2 mile for Goosenecks and 0.7 mile for Sunset Point round-trip

Hiking time: 15 minutes and 30 minutes, respectively

Difficulty: Easy

Trail surface: Packed dirt

Best season: Year-round

Other trail users: None

Fees and permits: No permit or fee required

Maps: Park map and brochure available at the visitor center

Trail contact: Capitol Reef National Park, HC 70, Box 15, Torrey, Utah, 84775; www.nps.gov/care

Finding the trailhead: The Panorama Point parking area is 2.4 miles west of the visitor center on Hwy. 24

The Hike

Visitors in a hurry to get a taste of what Utah's least-visited national park offers need to stop here for a glimpse. This is a stop many people simply traveling through the park without intentions to do any hiking will make to stretch their legs, snap a couple of pictures, and then jump back in the car to continue their adventure.

The Goosenecks is roughly a 1,200-foot round-trip walk to peer down into the goosenecks of Sulphur Creek. At 800 feet deep, the view is almost as long as the walk to see it. If your timing is good, you might catch a glimpse of people hiking though the canyon below as part of the Sulphur Creek hike—something much more adventurous visitors do. You may find Sulphur Creek calling to you

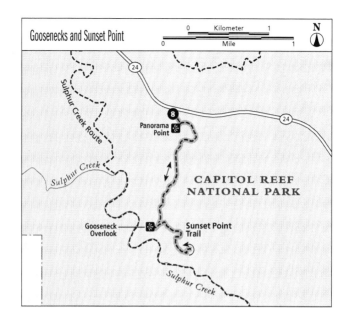

after peering down at it. Go for it; it is one of my favorite hikes in the park.

A sign for the Goosenecks is on the south end of the parking area and will help get you pointed in the right direction. Use caution when peering into the gorge Sulphur Creek has created. The rock can be slippery with sand on top.

Sunset Point is a short walk starting on the east side of the parking lot. A bench marks the midpoint of the walk. Another bench is located at the end of the trail to make taking in the sunset that much easier. Just as with the Goosenecks walk, use caution when hiking near the edge of the delicate cliffs.

As the name indicates, this is a great place for visitors to Capitol Reef National Park to be at sunset. The view takes in Fruita and beyond all the way to the Henry Mountains (not in the park) and includes Chimney Rock to the north.

Miles and Directions

0.0 In the Panorama Point parking area.

0.10 Goosenecks.

0.35 Sunset Point.

⑨ Fremont Gorge Overlook

Start: Blacksmith Shop parking lot on the Scenic Drive
Distance: 4.5 miles round-trip
Hiking time: 3–4 hours
Difficulty: Strenuous
Trail surface: Service road, loose gravel, packed dirt
Best season: Fall and spring
Other trail users: None

Fees and permits: No permit or fee required
Maps: Park map and brochure available at the visitor center
Trail contact: Capitol Reef National Park, HC 70, Box 15, Torrey, Utah, 84775; www.nps.gov/care

Finding the trailhead: The Blacksmith Shop parking lot is 0.8 of a mile south of the visitor center on the Scenic Drive. A sign for the Fremont Gorge Overlook Trail is on the west end of the parking area. The trail starts on a service road

The Hike

Trails on the campground side of the Fremont River in the Fruita District see a lot of traffic. Not so much on the other side of the river. The Fremont Gorge Overlook Trail is often overlooked when visitors plan their activities in the park.

Hikers heading away from the Blacksmith Shop will get a view of the Gifford House and barn and then the campground before making a turn to the right to follow a sign indicating the route. The trail leads to a flat known as Johnson Mesa. Visitors enter juniper stands about 1.2 miles from the trailhead. Soon the bulk of the elevation gain of more than a thousand feet is ahead.

At the 2-mile mark, the climbing has mellowed and visitors will pass the edge of the Fremont Gorge. The gorge is

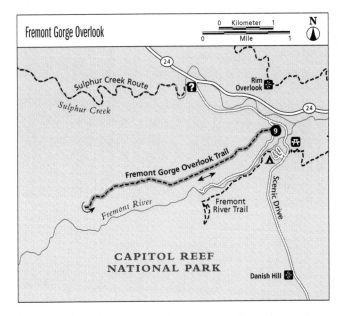

deep, rough, and extreme, quite a contrast from the environment hiked across to get to this point. Take a look at the river deep in the canyon and imagine that at one time it ran across the high country, eventually carving its way to the current depth. This land feels more rugged than the slickrock hikers walk on and through on most of the other hikes. The trail ends shortly after meeting the gorge.

Miles and Directions

0.0 Start at the Blacksmith Shop on the Scenic Drive south of the visitor center.

1.2 Enter juniper stands.

2.0 Brink of the Fremont Gorge.

2.4 End of the trail.

4.5 Arrive back at the Blacksmith Shop.

10 **Fremont River**

Start: Official start is along the Fremont River near the amphitheater and Loop B in the Fruita Campground
Distance: 2.2 miles
Hiking time: 2 hours
Difficulty: Moderate
Trail surface: Packed dirt
Best season: Year-round

Other trail users: None
Fees and permits: No permit or fees required
Maps: Park map and brochure available at the visitor center
Trail contact: Capitol Reef National Park, HC 70, Box 15, Torrey, Utah, 84775; www.nps. gov/care

Finding the trailhead: Drive 1.4 miles from the visitor center on the Scenic Drive. Turn right at the sign indicating Loop C of the campground and the Amphitheater sign. Continue straight past the entrance to Loop C on the right and orchards on the left. A gravel parking area is located at the end of the road.

The Hike

It is easy to see why pioneers were first drawn to the Fremont River in this desert landscape. It is truly an oasis, and the orchards that run along the river near the campground are a true wonder in such an extreme environment.

The trail is busy first thing in the morning or late in the evening as people camping or visiting the orchards take advantage of its location and squeeze in an "extra" hike among other plans. This is a family place with kids in carriers and those just learning how to walk. The Fremont River Trail is also accessible for people in wheelchairs before it makes a steep climb to the south. It is a nice stroll for people with limitations.

People not camping in Capitol Reef often park at the large picnic area on the Scenic Drive between the Ripple Rock Nature Center and the Gifford House.

It is a short walk to the Gifford House and you can pick up the trail along the Fremont there. Continuing south, you will walk past the A and B loops of the campground before reaching the amphitheater and the parking area accessed from the Loop C entrance from the Scenic Drive.

While walking along the campgrounds, keep an eye out for mule deer and wild turkeys. These animals are commonly spotted in the campground area and are accustomed to people, but they remain wild. Do not attempt to approach or feed the wildlife. Admire wild animals from a distance for your safety and for their safety. The deer can be particularly dangerous in the late fall during mating season. This is also the time of year the male deer, known as bucks, with large antlers will show up to mate with the females. They will sometimes battle each other for the right to pass on their genes. Their aggression can also be turned to visitors who get too close.

Chukars, ground birds named after their "chuk, chuk, chuk" call, are also often spotted in the campground, but

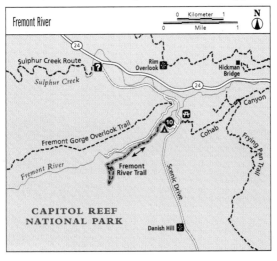

usually on the east side in the tent-only area and near the cliffs on the other side of the Scenic Drive. Once while camped in the "tent only" area of Fruita, I caught sight of a bright red creature moving in the trees. I studied the bird and later confirmed my suspicion with a park naturalist that it was a male vermillion flycatcher—a rare sighting in Utah.

The amphitheater, used for Ranger Talks during the busy season, serves as the official start of the hike. It also serves as an impromptu stage for families walking by. Many children have hopped up on the stage to do a quick performance for their family and friends during this hike.

The trail heads south against the flow of the Fremont River. Visitors will eventually cross a bridge and pass under large cottonwood trees. A horse pasture, sometimes with actual horses present, comes next. While it is fun to feed the horses apples from the orchards, it is better not to add to their diet. Rangers told us during one trip that so many people fed the horses apples that some became sick and required veterinary care. Avoid the temptation.

Passing the pasture, the start of the uphill portion of the hike awaits.

After a steady climb for about half a mile, hikers reach a switchback with a great view of the Fremont Gorge. The trail then heads east and south to a ridge at a gradual climb.

On top of the ridge is a cool view of the Waterpocket Fold to the east and many other popular Capitol Reef landmarks. Time to head back to camp for that freshly picked Dutch Oven apple cobbler.

Miles and Directions

- **0.0**   Start at the amphitheater.
- **1.1**   Reach the top of the trail.
- **2.2**   Arrive back at the amphitheater.

11 Cassidy Arch

Start: The Grand Wash Trailhead
Distance: 3.5 miles round-trip
Hiking time: 2–3 hours
Difficulty: Strenuous
Trail surface: Slickrock, sand
Best season: Year-round
Other trail users: Frying Pan Trail, Grand Wash
Fees and permits: An entrance fee is required to drive the Scenic Drive past the Fruita Campground. The permit, which is available for a fee for individuals (bicycles or pedestrians) and a slightly higher fee for vehicles, is good for 7 days
Maps: Park map and brochure available at the visitor center
Trail contact: Capitol Reef National Park, HC 70, Box 15, Torrey, Utah, 84775; www.nps.gov/care

Finding the trailhead: Take the Scenic Road to the Grand Wash dirt road. The trailhead is 1.25 miles after the turn. Start walking east along the wash and after 0.75 of a mile, you will come to a sign on the left indicating the start of the Cassidy Arch Trail

The Hike

It is entirely possible that the famous outlaw Butch Cassidy visited this arch, but it is much more likely that someone just wanted to name it after him.

There is no need to strap on chaps and spurs to do this hike, but you will want water and sunscreen. After leaving the Grand Wash Trailhead, hikers travel about three-fourths of a mile to the sign for Cassidy Arch.

The first portion of this trail can be a little intimidating, especially if you have a fear of heights. The initial 0.30 of a mile after the turn is steep and somewhat exposed, but the trail soon mellows out.

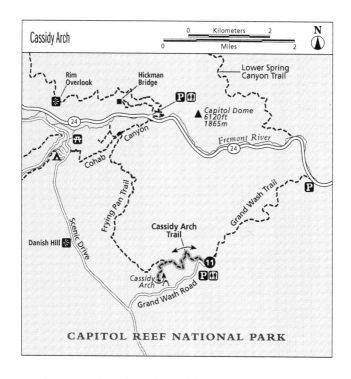

Hikers get their first view of the arch around the 1-mile mark. Soon after—at the 1.25-mile mark—you come to a sign marking the Frying Pan Trail (see the Frying Pan and Cohab Canyon trail descriptions for details on how these trails link). Go left at the sign to Cassidy Arch, which is 0.50 of a mile away.

Cassidy Arch is unique in that your approach takes you above the formation rather than below it. Cassidy Arch also seems a darker red than most other Utah arches.

Taking a break for water and looking down at the arch, you cannot help but wonder if Butch Cassidy ever did lay eyes on the formation and, if so, what may have been going through his mind while doing the same.

Miles and Directions

0.0   Start at the Grand Wash Trailhead.

0.75 Sign for Cassidy Arch on the left.

1.0   First glimpse of the arch.

1.25 Sign for Frying Pan Trail. Stay left.

3.5   Arrive back at the trailhead.

12 Chimney Rock

Start: Chimney Rock Trailhead on Hwy. 24

Distance: 3.5 miles loop

Hiking time: 3-4 hours

Difficulty: Strenuous

Trail surface: Clay, packed dirt

Best season: Year-round

Other trail users: Spring Canyon

Fees and permits: No fees or permits required

Maps: Park map and brochure available at the visitor center

Trail contact: Capitol Reef National Park, HC 70, Box 15, Torrey, Utah, 84775; www.nps. gov/care

Finding the trailhead: Chimney Rock Trailhead is on Hwy. 24, 3.1 miles west of the visitor center

The Hike

It can sometimes be difficult to understand how some rock formations were named. That is somewhat the case with Chimney Rock. From Hwy. 24 looking up you can kind of see a chimney. From the viewing points on the Chimney Rock Trail looking down, it is pretty obvious how this unique formation earned its name.

The trail starts on the north end of the parking area and feels like a small rollercoaster ride with rolling ups and downs before the serious part of the climb starts. After a brisk climb on switchbacks, hikers come to a fork in the trail about 0.50 of a mile from the trailhead.

This is the start of the loop. Turning left will take you away from Chimney Rock to Chimney Rock Canyon and Spring Canyon. This is an easier, but longer, route to the main destination of the hike—the southern edge viewing points. Most visitors turn right at the junction and head for the vistas.

The climbing continues, but it is not long before the reward comes. The first viewpoint is a long patio on the cliff edge with a big view to the south and west looking toward Boulder Mountain in the distance. Just a little further up the trail is the high point of the loop. The view is spectacular to the south and east. Waterpocket Fold and the Henry Mountains make up most of the vast skyline.

Once you have taken in the views and filled your memory card with images, the loop trail continues to the east and starts to drop gradually. You will get a peek at the Capitol Reef National Park Visitor Center and the Fruit District.

The trail eventually meets another junction roughly 2.2 miles into the hike. Turning right leads hikers into Spring

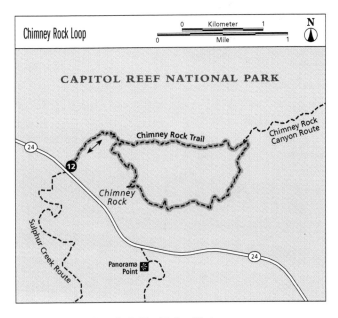

Canyon. Staying on course (mostly west) will get you back to the trailhead.

The lower sections of the trail comprise clay. Expect a sticky, slippery, muddy mess if the trail is wet. This clay sticks to everything. The good news is you will have traces of it in your vehicle months after the adventure, which, hopefully, brings back fond memories.

Miles and Directions

0.0 Start at the Chimney Rock Trailhead.

0.5 Start of the loop, most people.

0.75 First real viewing stop.

1.0 Another viewing point.

2.2 Junction to Spring Canyon.

3.5 Arrive back at the trailhead.

13 Navajo Knobs

Start: Hickman Bridge Trailhead on Hwy. 24
Distance: 9.3 miles round-trip
Hiking time: 6–7 hours
Difficulty: Strenuous
Trail surface: Packed dirt, slickrock
Best season: Spring and fall
Other trail users: Hickman Bridge, Rim Overlook

Fees and permits: No permit required
Maps: Park map and brochure available at the visitor center
Trail contact: Capitol Reef National Park, HC 70, Box 15, Torrey, Utah, 84775; www.nps.gov/care

Finding the trailhead: The Hickman Bridge Trailhead is 1.9 miles east of the visitor center on Hwy. 24

The Hike

The Navajo Knobs Trail leads hikers into the most remote country of all the Fruita District opportunities. At more than 9 miles it turns off most day-trippers and gives visitors who do make the trek a true chance at solitude.

Please see the Hickman Bridge and Rim Overlook trail descriptions before reading details on the Navajo Knobs portion of the trail.

Most people making this journey are doing so for the vaunted panoramic views associated with this part of Capitol Reef.

About two-thirds of a mile from the Rim Overlook, the trail starts a long descent. Another ascent and short descent leads to the last mile to Navajo Knobs. A special look into the north country of the park is granted to hikers who complete the journey.

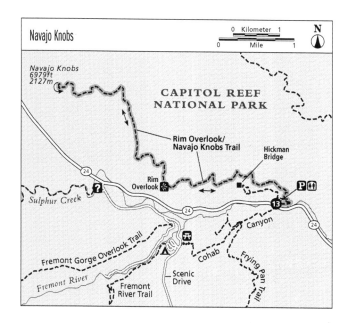

When the air is clear, and it is most days, notable landmarks within the site include the LaSal Mountains near Moab and Factory Butte on the San Rafael Swell.

Before starting back, take time to explore the area around and on the Knobs.

Remember most of the return is downhill. Take a break when you get to the Hickman Bridge Overlook and see how different it looks later in the day. Lighting is one of the greatest mysteries of the desert and why every trip can feel like a new adventure.

Miles and Directions

0.0 Start at the Hickman Bridge Trailhead on Hwy. 24.

0.3 Arrive at the junction to Hickman Bridge. Stay right for the Rim Overlook and Navajo Knobs destinations.

2.2 Approximate halfway point at Rim Overlook viewpoint.

4.65 Reach the Navajo Knobs.

9.3 Arrive back at the trailhead.

14 Frying Pan

Start: Connects Cassidy Arch and Cohab Canyon trails
Distance: 3.5 miles
Hiking time: 4–5 hours if hiking the trail from one point to another
Difficulty: Strenuous
Trail surface: Packed dirt, slickrock
Best season: Year-round
Other trail users: Cohab Canyon, Cassidy Arch
Fees and permits: An entrance fee is required to drive the Scenic Drive past the Fruita Campground. The permit, which is available for a fee for individuals (bicycles or pedestrians) and a slightly higher fee for vehicles, is good for 7 days. A permit is not required for starting from the Cohab Canyon Trail
Maps: Park map and brochure available at the visitor center
Trail contact: Capitol Reef National Park, HC 70, Box 15, Torrey, Utah, 84775; www.nps.gov/care

Finding the trailhead: One end of the Frying Pan Trail is 1.25 miles on the Cassidy Arch Trail from the Grand Wash Trailhead, while the other is 1 mile on the Cohab Canyon Trailhead starting near the Fruita Campground

The Hike

This trail could easily be just an extension of either Cohab Canyon or Cassidy Arch. Maybe somebody decided to give the middle portion a different name after a hike on an extremely hot day.

Whatever the source of the name, the Frying Pan Trail is worth a visit. Many people do a point-to-point over the Frying Pan for a long day hike. Most catch a ride to the Grand Wash Trailhead, visit Cassidy Arch, and then follow

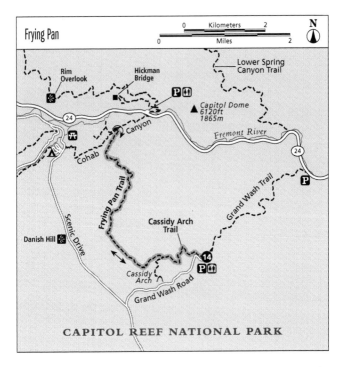

Frying Pan

0   Kilometers   2

0   Miles   2

N

Rim
Overlook

Hickman
Bridge

Lower Spring
Canyon Trail

🅿 🚻

Capitol Dome
6120ft
1865m

24

Canyon

Fremont River

24

🅿

🏕

Cohab

🏕

Frying Pan Trail

Danish Hill

Scenic Drive

Cassidy Arch
Trail

Grand Wash Trail

🅿

14

🅿 🚻

Cassidy
Arch

Grand Wash Road

CAPITOL REEF NATIONAL PARK

the Frying Pan to Cohab Canyon and walk to their site at the
campground. This is not a casual hike with an overall elevation gain of more than a thousand feet. The highest point is
about a mile north from the Cassidy Arch junction.

If you have not seen Cassidy Arch, there really is no reason not to make the side trip if hiking Frying Pan Trail. It is
worth the time and effort to see the natural red rock arch.

Look for a wash crossing the trail about 1 mile past the
highest point. Wander down the wash a bit and check out
some tanks below.

Another 1.5 miles and hikers will come to the Cohab
Canyon Trail. If you turn left, it is a mile to the Fruita

Campground. If you turn right, it is 0.7 of a mile to the Hickman Bridge parking area.

A short spur on the Cohab Trail heads to the north soon after the junction from the Frying Pan. The Fruita Overlook trail leads to two overlooks and adds about 1.2 miles to the hike.

Make sure to read about the Cohab Canyon hike if doing Frying Pan. Plan on extra time for this hike if you have kids. They will be drawn to dipping their toes into the fine, cool sand of Cohab Canyon and will find the red rock viewing portals too much to resist.

Miles and Directions

0.0 Frying Pan starts on the Cassidy Arch Trail about 1.25 miles from the Grand Wash Trailhead.

1.0 The highest point of the hike.

2.0 A sandy wash crosses the trail.

3.5 Junction with Cohab Canyon Trail.

15 **Sulphur Creek**

Start: Chimney Rock parking area on Hwy. 24

Distance: 5.8 miles

Hiking time: The Sulphur Creek hike takes 4 to 5 hours

Difficulty: Strenuous

Trail surface: Packed dirt, slickrock, stream bed, sand

Best season: Spring, summer, and fall

Other trail users: None

Fees and permits: No fees or permits required

Maps: Park map and brochure available at the visitor center

Trail contact: Capitol Reef National Park, HC 70, Box 15, Torrey, Utah, 84775; www.nps.gov/care

---

Finding the trailhead: Parking is available at Chimney Rock Trailhead 3.1 miles west of the visitor center. The trail starts across from the parking area on the south side of Hwy. 24. It is also possible to start at the visitor center and hike up Sulphur Creek. It is a good idea to arrange a ride or drop a car off before starting this hike

The Hike

Sulphur Creek is not a marked or maintained trail, but enough people have done the hike that it is quite easy to follow. Besides, it is a slot canyon—where else can you go?

People have been doing the Sulphur Creek hike for years, but its popularity has increased exponentially in the past decade. The hike represents a small taste of canyoneering and is popular with large groups and families.

Sulphur Creek is a perennial stream—meaning it has a constant flow of water throughout the year—that enters Capitol Reef National Park from the west. In fact, visitors coming from Torrey on Hwy. 24 drive over the creek.

This is a perfect hike for the hottest days, as it offers immediate relief from the heat. It is *not* the place to be in if there is a possibility of a flash flood. Check the weather at the visitor center before setting off on this hike.

Wear shoes that offer support, but ones that can get wet. There are multiple places where you will need to cross the creek. While most of the time the creek is easily jumped across, hikers will almost always fully submerse their feet—and maybe even have to swim in some conditions—at the obstacle lowest on the hike. Be careful walking along the creek; algae growth can make some areas particularly slippery. Hiking out with a twisted ankle or injured knee or back is not easy.

After crossing the highway from the Chimney Rock parking area, look for a narrow trail heading south. It quickly enters a wash. Follow the wash to a larger wash and head down it for 1.4 miles. The wash will get continually narrower before hikers reach a set of 6-foot pour-offs.

Sulphur Creek is not far now. Once there, turn left and walk downstream. It may become necessary to cross the stream to continue down the canyon. After about half a mile, look up. The canyon is now 800 feet deep. Smile, visitors at the Goosenecks Overlook might be watching you.

Continue walking for another mile to the first falls and official start of the narrows portion of the Sulphur Creek hike. First is a steep 10-foot pitch that usually requires people to use their arms and legs in descent. About 750 feet below is another waterfall.

The final obstacle is 1.7 miles downstream. The roughly 8-foot waterfall presents a slippery option to get past. If the water is high and you are not prepared for a swim, there is an out.

Some have started a bypass trail about 20 yards above the waterfall and it is possible to get out of the narrows on the south side of the canyon. The trail eventually leads back to the creek quite a ways from the waterfall.

The rest of the hike is 0.7 of a mile to Hwy. 24 and the visitor center. A fun destination is found on the left side of the canyon where the cliffs stop. Look for the limekiln built by early settlers of Fruita.

The hike is not for young children, although some adventurous 6-year-olds might be able to handle it. Many families walk upstream from the visitor center to the first obstacle, a small waterfall. The hike is about 0.7 of a mile.

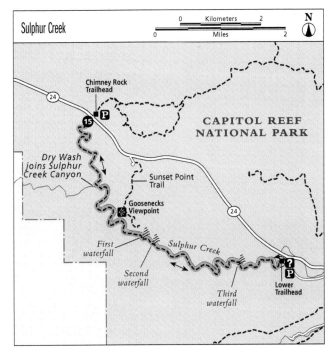

Kids love walking in the water and, depending on what flash floods have done to change things, there might be a pool to play in at the waterfall.

Miles and Directions

- **0.0** Start at the Chimney Rock parking area and cross Hwy. 24 to the south to start the hike.
- **1.4** Arrive at two 6-foot pour offs.
- **1.9** Look up 800 feet to the Goosenecks Overlook.
- **2.9** First obstacle and start of the narrows.
- **4.6** Final obstacle.
- **5.5** Capitol Reef National Park Visitor center.

WATERPOCKET FOLD

The Waterpocket Fold is a distinctive geological formation most obvious on the east side of Capitol Reef National Park. The warp in the earth's crust runs roughly 100 miles, with one quite steep uplift. The Waterpocket Fold has tilted layers of the earth ranging from 80 million years to 275 million years ago. The oldest layers are on the west side of the Waterpocket Fold, with the youngest layers on the eastern side. Day hikes in the Waterpocket fold tend to be in slot canyons and offer visitors a chance to visit remote locations. The Waterpocket Fold hikes are accessed via the Notom–Bullfrog Road about nine miles east of the visitor center and south of Hwy. 24. The first 5 miles of the Notom–Bullfrog Road are paved. Cars with good clearance should not have a problem reaching the trailheads. Always be prepared for flash floods on the Notom Road. If water is flowing over the road, do not assume it is okay to drive through. There may be holes in the road created by the flash flood.

16 Headquarters Canyon

Start: Headquarters Canyon
Trailhead
Distance: 3.2 miles
Hiking time: 2.5-3 hours
Difficulty: Moderate
Trail surface: Packed dirt, sand,
slickrock
Best season: Spring, summer,
and fall

Other trail users: None
Fees and permits: No fees or
permits required
Maps: Park map and brochure
available at the visitor center
Trail contact: Capitol Reef
National Park, HC 70, Box 15,
Torrey, Utah, 84775; www.nps.
gov/care

Finding the trailhead: Travel the Notom-Bullfrog Road roughly 2.3
miles south past the Burr Trail intersection. A parking lot near the Post
Corral is on the left and across the road to the Muley Twist trailhead.
Park and cross the road. Follow the fence line on the left side to a
sign for Headquarters Canyon

The Hike

In his book, Stinchfield says that while the hike does include
a long drive on a dirt road, Headquarters Canyon is "probably the most accessible good slot canyon in the park." It is
on the radar of most adventurous families with young children because it is an easy hike with no obstacles.

The Post Corral, which serves as the trailhead, was a stopping point for ranchers moving cattle through the desert on
the east side of what is now known as Capitol Reef National
Park.

A hike across a flat leads to the mouth of the canyon.
Keep an eye out for cairns to help find the way. The entrance
to the canyon is about 0.75 of a mile from the trailhead.

It is not long before hikers reach a steep and narrow slot in Headquarters Canyon. The canyon at this point is only about shoulder-width apart for about 200 feet.

Headquarters Canyon remains narrow as you continue up the trail, but not quite as tight. About 1.5 miles from the road the sand wash bottom ends and slickrock begins.

Visitors will hike only a little ways longer before the trail ends at a pour-off obstacle.

Headquarters Canyon offers a great opportunity to talk to kids about the unique geology of Capitol Reef. Sandstone formations visible during the hike include Entrada, Carmel formation, Kayenta, and Windgate. To make it a full day,

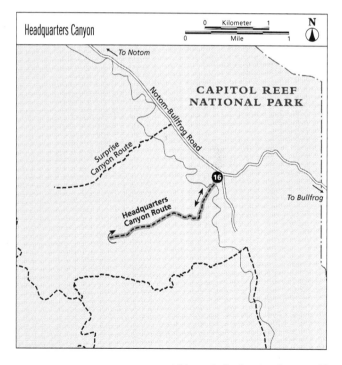

consider combining the Headquarters Canyon hike with the Surprise Canyon hike.

Miles and Directions

0.0 Start at the Post Corral parking area.

0.75 Enter the canyon.

1.5 End of the trail.

3.2 Arrive back at the trailhead.

17 Surprise Canyon

Start: Surprise Canyon Trailhead
Distance: 2 miles
Hiking time: 1-2 hours
Difficulty: Easy
Trail surface: Packed dirt, sand, slickrock
Best season: Year-round
Other trail users: None

Fees and permits: No fees or permits required
Maps: Park map and brochure available at the visitor center
Trail contact: Capitol Reef National Park, HC 70, Box 15, Torrey, Utah, 84775; www.nps. gov/care

Finding the trailhead: Look for a small parking lot off the Notom-Bullfrog Road about 1.8 miles south of the Burr Trail intersection

The Hike

Most people visiting this remote portion of the park have their minds set on serious backcountry or slot canyon adventures. As a result, most visitors bypass this "easy" hike, and the chances of a quiet walk are high. That is if the kids can contain themselves. It is a long ride from the "developed" side of Capitol Reef and by the time the kids get out of the car for the Surprise Canyon hike they should be raring to go.

There is no elevation gain on the 1-mile out-and-back hike. This is a wonderful place to soak up the desert environment—the geological formations and the unique fauna of the region.

The trail starts by crossing a flat to the canyon. About 0.2 of a mile in the hike, the trail crosses Halls Creek. The trail can get lost in the sand and changing vegetation. Aim for the mouth of the canyon, which is easy to see from the trailhead.

The walls are steep in Surprise Canyon and the trail lasts only about 1 mile from the trailhead before a chockstone blocks the way. There is a route around the obstacle, but not much else to see before another, more major, obstacle ends the trip.

Consider making the drive worth it and haul the kids the short distance to check out Headquarters Canyon for another adventure.

Miles and Directions

0.0 Start at the Surprise Canyon Trailhead.

0.2 Cross Halls Creek.

1.0 End of the trail.

2.0 Arrive back at the trailhead.

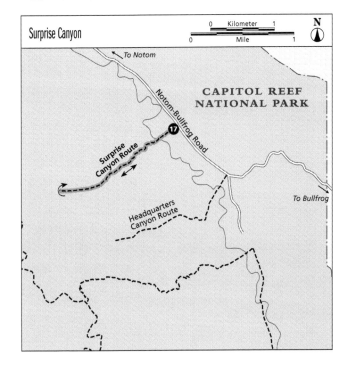

18 Burro Wash

Start: A pullout on the
Notom-Bullfrog Road 7.6 miles
south of Hwy. 24
Distance: 7.5 miles
Hiking time: 4–6 hours
Difficulty: Strenuous
Trail surface: Sand, slickrock
Best season: Year-round
Other trail users: None

Fees and permits: No fees or
permits required
Maps: Park map and brochure
available at the visitor center
Trail contact: Capitol Reef
National Park, HC 70, Box 15,
Torrey, Utah, 84775; www.nps.
gov/care

Finding the trailhead: Head 9 miles east of the visitor center on
Hwy. 24 to the Notom-Bullfrog Road turnoff. A large pullout is on the
right hand side of the road at 7.6 miles. There should be a small sign
at the pullout

The Hike

Burro Wash is the most northern of the major slot canyon hikes on the east side of Capitol Reef National Park.
This truly is a strenuous hike with some serious scrambling
skills required. This is not for sandal-wearing, store-bought-
10-ounce-water-bottle-carrying tourists but for educated
and careful hikers. Park officials want visitors to be aware
that the slot canyon hikes in the national park are not trails
by definition, but routes which can change due to a number
of factors.

Hikers should be prepared to get wet as conditions in
the canyon change with each major rain storm. Sections dry
on one hike could be under a couple of feet of water the
next time.

The first 2 miles of the route follows a dry streambed—unless monsoon rains have filled it to the banks with water and debris. No need to mention you should not enter any slot canyon in Capitol Reef during a storm or if rain is forecast.

The Bureau of Land Management administers the first portion of the trail. The sand can be deep in places and it is likely you will be carrying some of the grains home with you at the end of the day. The streambed is lined with large cottonwood trees and it eventually narrows to the slot canyon. The footing also changes to a combination of sand and slickrock.

The National Park Service boundary for Capitol Reef National Park is about two miles up the wash. The last realistic parking area for cars driving up the streambed is about half a mile from the true start of the canyon.

Shortly after crossing into the park the canyon divides, take the right fork and you soon come to the first obstacle. This one does not present much of a delay.

Hikers then come to the first slot in Burro Wash. The chockstone at the next obstacle is a little more substantial, but once one person is up the boulder they should be able to provide help.

Make sure to scan the walls of the canyon, particularly in the more open areas, for petroglyphs. Bighorn sheep may also be spotted while hiking Burro Wash.

The next challenge requires spider walking—all four limbs—and some help from friction on the side walls.

Two large boulders make the next barriers in Burro. This is a challenging obstacle and some people turn around here. If you make it past the two boulders, there are a few minor

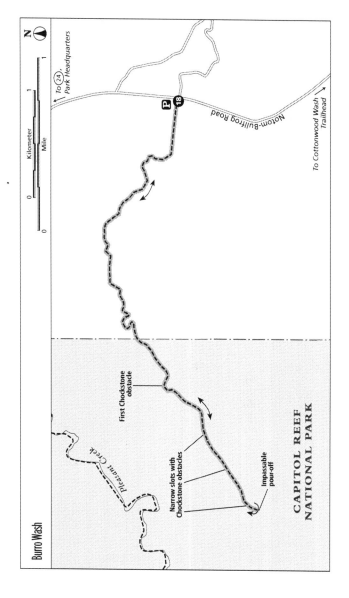

Burro Wash

Pleasant Creek

First Chockstone obstacle

Narrow slots with Chockstone obstacles

Impassable pour-off

CAPITOL REEF NATIONAL PARK

Notom-Bullfrog Road

P

18

To 24, Park Headquarters

To Cottonwood Wash Trailhead

N

Kilometer

Mile

0   1

0   1

obstacles—if there has not been an altering flash flood—before reaching the end of Burro Wash. A pour-off way out of reach marks the end.

Miles and Directions

0.0   Start on the Notom-Bullfrog Road at the Burro Wash Trailhead marker.

2.0   National Park Service boundary marker.

3.75 End of the Burro Wash trail.

7.5   Arrive back at the trailhead.

19 Cottonwood Wash

Start: Cottonwood Wash Trailhead off the Notom-Bullfrog road
Distance: 6.0 miles
Hiking time: 4–6 hours
Difficulty: Strenuous
Trail surface: Sand and slickrock
Best season: Year-round
Other trail users: None

Fees and permits: No fees or permits required
Maps: Park map and brochure available at the visitor center
Trail contact: Capitol Reef National Park, HC 70, Box 15, Torrey, Utah, 84775; www.nps.gov/care

Finding the trailhead: Cottonwood Wash is the middle of the three main slot canyons on the east side of the park. The trailhead is 8.9 miles south of Hwy. 24 on the Notom-Bullfrog Road. There is parking off the highway and some shade provided by large Cottonwood trees

The Hike

There is no significant difference in the three main slot canyons on the east side of Capitol Reef, but it seems like this one gets most of the love. Likely because it is the shortest. But, as is the case with the majority of hikes in the park, you can make them as long or as short as you like.

That being said, hikes on the east side of the national park see a fraction of visitors compared to those on the western portion of Capitol Reef.

From the parking area along the Notom Road, follow the wash west. You may pass people who have set up camp in the riverbed. It is possible to drive up the wash with a four-wheel-drive vehicle, but most people use the main parking area near the road.

Follow the wash west from the parking area for 1.2 miles to where the canyon starts to narrow. Hikers get two narrow stretches of canyon before the true obstacles start—at least at this writing. Conditions in all Utah desert canyons can change with every storm. What one day might be an easy jaunt up the canyon can become a technical climb after a flood event. Another storm a week later could change things again.

We actually climbed under wedged rocks to pass one obstacle—try doing this without thinking of Aron Ralston.

We met the end of our hike in Cottonwood after coming across a long, deep, and cold pool of water under a large chockstone. The pool was wadeable, but it was impossible to climb over the chockstone without gear. There are reports of this pool being more than 10 feet deep in certain conditions.

Those prepared to handle the obstacle, which should only be attempted by experienced canyoneers, will be rewarded, according to Stinchfield.

There is a unique pothole just past the major obstacle and then "a long, slanted, narrow slot that may be the best section on the hike," Stinchfield wrote in *Capitol Reef National Park: The Complete Hiking and Touring Guide.*

There may be more pools to deal with before coming to a true end to the Cottonwoood Wash hike—a 10-foot dryfall.

Miles and Directions

0.0 Start at the parking area just off the Notom-Bullfrog Road 8.9 miles south of Hwy. 24.

1.2 The wash narrows considerably.

3.01 Likely end for most people with a deep pool and high chockstone.

6.0 Arrive back at the parking area.

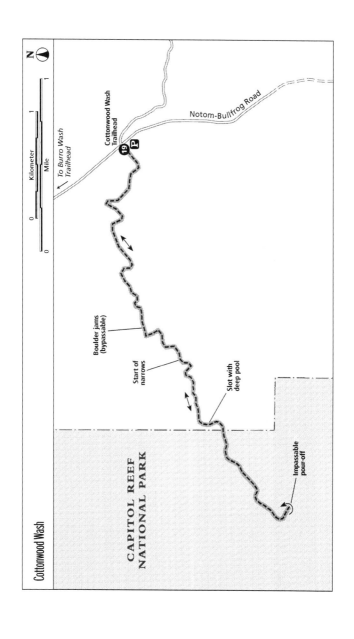

Cottonwood Wash

N

Kilometer

Mile

To Burro Wash Trailhead

Cottonwood Wash Trailhead

19 P

Notom-Bullfrog Road

Boulder jams (bypassable)

Start of narrows

Slot with deep pool

CAPITOL REEF NATIONAL PARK

Impassable pour-off

20 Sheets Gulch

Start: Sheets Gulch Trailhead off the Notom-Bullfrog Road
Distance: 13.8 miles
Hiking time: 7–8 hours
Difficulty: Strenuous
Trail surface: Sand, slickrock
Best season: Year-round
Other trail users: Tantalus Flats

Fees and permits: No fees or permits required
Maps: Park map and brochure available at the visitor center
Trail contact: Capitol Reef National Park, HC 70, Box 15, Torrey, Utah, 84775; www.nps.gov/care

Finding the trailhead: The Sheets Gulch parking area is 12.7 miles south of Hwy. 24 on the Notom-Bullfrog Road. The parking is just off the road

The Hike

Sheets is the most southern of the three popular canyons on the east side of Capitol Reef National Park and accessed through the Notom-Bullfrog Road. Sheets is longer than the other two but usually lacks the major obstacles in the others. Flash flood events could easily alter the hike and make it a true obstacle course, so be prepared for anything.

A walk just over a mile in the sandy wash leads to the start of the canyon. Visitors will pass through one narrow and then hit a longer slot about 2.25 miles into the hike.

A large boulder sits in the path 4.5 miles into the hike but usually does not prove difficult to get past.

Sheets Gulch then takes on a different feel from many other Capitol Reef hikes with the appearance of Douglas firs. The hiking is easier here and it would probably be easy to hike on, but in *Capitol Reef National Park: The Complete*

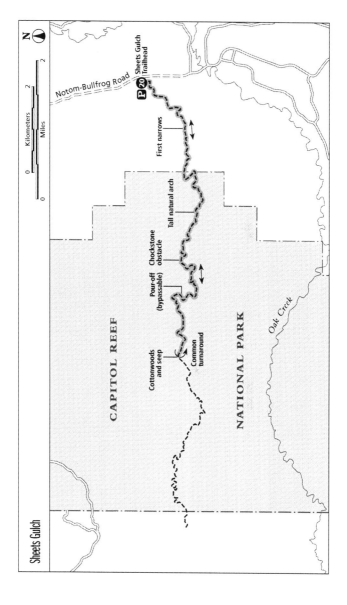

Sheets Gulch

Hiking and Touring Guide Stinchfield says there is not much reason to continue and suggests hikers turn back at the 6.8-mile mark. Stinchfield said the only reason to keep going would be if a car were waiting at Tantalus Flats. Otherwise, it makes sense to turn around and enjoy the walk back.

Miles and Directions

0.0   Start on the Notom-Bullfrog Road at the Burro Wash Trailhead marker.

1.2   Start of the canyon.

2.25 Start of a long slot.

4.5   Large chock boulder.

6.8   A likely turnaround location.

13.8 Arrive back at the trailhead.

CATHEDRAL DISTRICT

Few people realize there is a largely unvisited portion of the park to the north. Even fewer actually make the trip to visit the remote backcountry area known as the Cathedral District. This is no country for minivans, although some people successfully navigate the backcountry roads.

High-clearance vehicles are highly recommended when heading to the Cathedral Valley and four-wheel drive is highly encouraged. Access to the Cathedral District is limited to dirt roads, which may become impassable even to four-wheel drive vehicles when wet.

There are six hikes recognized by the National Park Service in the Cathedral District. All can be done as day hikes and it would be possible to do all six in a long weekend of exploring this unique landscape of monoliths and contrasting wide-open spaces.

Notable monoliths in the Cathedral District include Temple Rock, Temple of the Moon, and Temple of the Sun—soaring to 500 feet high from the desert floor. Other recognized landmarks include the Walls of Jericho, Glass Mountain, and the Gypsum Sinkhole. The sinkhole is a collapse in a gypsum deposit that left a 50-foot wide and 200-foot deep hole.

Some visitors comment the Cathedral Valley area of Capitol Reef National Park must look similar to what they imagine the surface of the planet Mars looks like.

They are not alone. Back in 2001, the Mars Desert Research Station was established on Bureau of Land Management lands just east of the Cathedral District of the national park. The station includes four buildings simulating possible living structures for a hoped-for mission to Mars. Researchers spend 2–3 weeks in the buildings. The location was selected for its remoteness and Mars-like environment.

Most visitors heading into the Cathedral District take the 57.6-mile Cathedral Valley Loop. The Loop, which provides access to the recognized hikes in the district, starts on the Hartnet Road, which begins 11.7 miles east of the visitor center on Hwy. 24.

Drive 27.8 miles to the Hartnet Junction and then turn north (right) onto Cathedral Road. It is 29.9 miles back to Hwy. 24. Caution—a ford across the Fremont River is required at the south end of the Hartnet Road close to Hwy. 24. Do not attempt the crossing during floods or high runoff.

Research a trip into the Cathedral District before making the journey. Details are provided on the park's website. Make sure to stop at the visitor center for a weather report and any new information before crossing the Fremont River and starting your adventure.

21 Cathedrals Trail

Start: Cathedrals Trailhead on the Cathedral Road
Distance: 2.4 miles
Hiking time: 1-2 hours
Difficulty: Easy
Trail surface: Packed dirt, sand
Best season: Spring and summer
Other trail users: None

Fees and permits: No fees or permits required
Maps: Park map and brochure available at the visitor center
Trail contact: Capitol Reef National Park, HC 70, Box 15, Torrey, Utah, 84775; www.nps. gov/care

Finding the trailhead: The trailhead is 27.4 miles from Hwy. 24 on the Cathedral Road or 2.4 miles north of the Hartnet Road Junction

The Hike

Hikers move along the edge of the massive monoliths known as the Cathedrals. A sign marks the start of the trail. There is a short ascent and then a mostly level walk before reaching the ridge. A hill makes the perfect perch to take in the Cathedrals and the Upper Cathedral Valley.

Do not just take one picture of this amazing scenery. Light is constantly changing the tones of the landscape. Many photographers utilize time-lapse functions and create slide-shows to illustrate the changing moods of the Capitol Reef desert and its impressive natural formations.

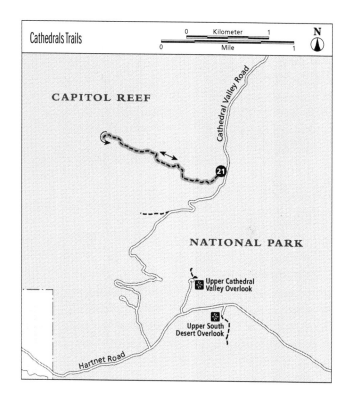

Cathedrals Trails

0 — Kilometer — 1

0 — Mile — 1

N

CAPITOL REEF

Cathedral Valley Road

21

NATIONAL PARK

Upper Cathedral
Valley Overlook

Upper South
Desert Overlook

Hartnet Road

Miles and Directions

0.0   Start at the Cathedrals Trailhead.

1.2   Hike up a small hill to take in the views.

2.4   Arrive back at the trailhead.

22 Lower Cathedral Valley Overlooks

Start: Lower Cathedral Valley Overlook Trailhead along the Hartnet Road
Distance: 1.5-2.5 miles
Hiking time: 1-2 hours
Difficulty: Moderate
Trail surface: Packed dirt, sand
Best season: Spring and fall
Other trail users: None

Fees and permits: No fees or permits required
Maps: Park map and brochure available at the visitor center
Trail contact: Capitol Reef National Park, HC 70, Box 15, Torrey, Utah, 84775; www.nps. gov/care

Finding the trailhead: The trailhead is on the Hartnet Road 17.6 miles from Hwy. 24

The Hike

This is the place to be if you want an amazing view of the iconic Temples of the Sun and Moon landmarks at Capitol Reef National Park.

These formations seem to rise from the ground like the tip of a giant sword or arrow point. They do not seem real, particularly when the moody light of the Utah desert makes them glow.

A diagram on a sign of the ridge marks the beginning of the trail. Hikers should follow a path north across a flat. There is a short, but steep, climb to a saddle with a rewarding view to the north of the Lower Cathedral Valley. Another saddle to the east with a good viewpoint can be reached after returning to the base of the cliffs. A trail may not be seen, but travel to the other saddle is allowed. Park officials say it is about 0.9 of a mile between the saddles.

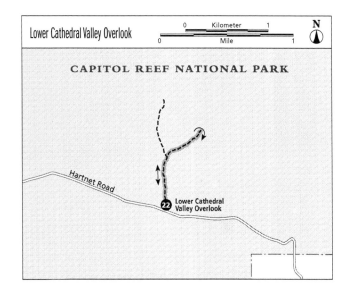

Lower Cathedral Valley Overlook

CAPITOL REEF NATIONAL PARK

Hartnet Road

22 Lower Cathedral Valley Overlook

Miles and Directions

0.0 Start at the Cathedral Valley Trailhead.

1.25 Stand in the second saddle and take in the view.

2.5 Arrive back at the trailhead.

The Art of Hiking

When standing nose-to-nose with a mountain lion, you are probably not too concerned with the issue of ethical behavior in the wild. No doubt, you are just terrified. But, let us be honest. How often are you nose-to-nose with a mountain lion? For most of us, a hike into the "wild" means loading up the SUV with expensive gear and driving to a toileted trailhead. Sure, you can mourn how civilized we have become—how global positioning system (GPS) units have replaced natural instinct and Gore-Tex stands in for true grit—but the silly gadgets of civilization aside, we have plenty of reasons to take pride in how we have matured. With survival now on the back burner, we have begun to understand that we have a responsibility to protect, no longer just conquer, our wild places—that they, not we, are at risk. So please, do what you can. The following section will help you understand better what it means to "do what you can" while still making the most of your hiking experience. Anyone can take a hike, but hiking safely and well is an art requiring preparation and proper equipment.

Trail Etiquette

Leave no trace. Always leave an area just like you found it—if not better than you found it. Avoid camping in fragile, alpine meadows and along the banks of streams and lakes. Use a camp stove versus building a wood fire. Pack up all of your trash and extra food. Bury human waste at least 100 feet from water sources under 6–8 inches of topsoil. Do not bathe with soap in a lake or stream—use prepackaged moistened towels to wipe off sweat and dirt, or bathe in the water without soap.

Stay on the trail. It is true, a path anywhere leads nowhere new, but purists will just have to get over it. Paths serve an important purpose: they limit impact on natural areas. Straying from a designated trail may seem innocent but it can cause damage to sensitive areas—damage that may take years to recover, if it can recover at all. Even simple shortcuts can be destructive. So, please, stay on the trail.

Leave no weeds. Noxious weeds tend to overtake other plants, which in turn affects animals and birds that depend on them for food. To minimize the spread of noxious weeds, hikers should regularly clean their boots, tents, packs, and hiking poles of mud and seeds. Also, brush your dog to remove any weed seeds before heading off into a new area.

Keep your dog under control. You can buy a flexi-lead that allows your dog to go exploring along the trail, while allowing you the ability to reel him in should another hiker approach or should he decide to chase a rabbit. Always obey leash laws and be sure to bury your dog's waste or pack it in resealable plastic bags.

Respect other trail users. Often you are not the only one on the trail. With the rise in popularity of multiuse trails, you will have to learn a new kind of respect, beyond the nod and "hello" approach you may be used to. First, investigate whether you are on a multiuse trail, and assume the appropriate precautions. When you encounter motorized vehicles (ATVs, motorcycles, and 4WDs), be alert. Though they should always yield to the hiker, often they are going too fast or are too lost in the buzz of their engine to react to your presence. If you hear activity ahead, step off the trail just to be safe. Note that you are not likely to hear a mountain biker coming, so be prepared, and know ahead of time whether you share the trail with them. Cyclists should always yield to hikers, but that is little comfort to the hiker. Be aware. When you approach horses or pack animals on the trail, always step quietly off the trail, preferably on the downhill side, and let them pass. If you are wearing a large backpack, it is often a good idea to sit down. To some animals, a hiker wearing a large backpack might appear threatening. Many national forests allow domesticated grazing, usually for sheep and cattle. Make sure your dog does not harass these animals, and respect ranchers' rights while you are enjoying yours.

Getting into Shape

Unless you want to be sore—and possibly have to shorten your trip or vacation—be sure to get in shape before a big hike. If you are terribly out of shape, start a walking program early, preferably eight weeks in advance. Start with a fifteen-minute walk during your lunch hour or after work and gradually increase your walking time to an hour. You should also increase your elevation gain. Walking briskly up hills really strengthens your leg muscles and gets your heart rate up. If you work in a storied office building, take the stairs instead of the elevator. If you prefer going to a gym, walk the treadmill or use a stair machine. You can further increase your strength and endurance by walking with a loaded backpack. Stationary exercises you might consider are squats, leg lifts, sit-ups, and push-ups. Other good ways to get in shape include biking, running, aerobics, and, of course, short hikes. Stretching before and after a hike keeps muscles flexible and helps avoid injuries.

Preparedness

It has been said that failing to plan means planning to fail. So do take the necessary time to plan your trip. Whether going on a short day hike or an extended backpack trip, always prepare for the worst. Simply remembering to pack a copy of the US Army Survival Manual is not preparedness. Although it is not a bad idea if you plan on entering truly wild places, it is merely the tourniquet answer to a problem. You need to do your best to prevent the problem from arising in the first place. In order to survive—and to stay reasonably comfortable—you need to concern yourself with the basics: water, food, and shelter. Do not go on a hike without having these bases covered. And, do not go on a hike expecting to find these items in the woods.

Water. Even in frigid conditions, you need at least two quarts of water a day to function efficiently. Add heat and taxing terrain and you can bump that figure up to one gallon. That is simply a base to work from—your metabolism and your level of conditioning can raise or lower that amount. Unless you know your level, assume that you need one gallon of water a day. Now, where do you plan on getting the water?

Preferably not from natural water sources. These sources can be loaded with intestinal disturbers, such as bacteria, viruses, and fertilizers. *Giardia lamblia,* the most common of these disturbers, is a protozoan parasite that lives part of its life cycle as a cyst in water sources. The parasite spreads when mammals defecate in water sources. Once ingested, Giardia can induce cramping, diarrhea, vomiting, and fatigue within two days to two weeks after ingestion. Giardiasis is treatable with prescription drugs. If you believe you have contracted giardiasis, see a doctor immediately.

Treating water. The best and easiest solution to avoid polluted water is to carry your water with you. Yet, depending on the nature of your hike and the duration, this may not be an option—one gallon of water weighs eight-and-a-half pounds. In that case, you will need to look into treating water. Regardless of which method you choose, you should always carry some water with you in case of an emergency. Save this reserve until you absolutely need it.

There are three methods of treating water: boiling, chemical treatment, and filtering. If you boil water, it is recommended that you do so for ten to fifteen minutes. This is often impractical because you are forced to exhaust a great deal of your fuel supply. You can opt for chemical treatment, which will kill Giardia but will not take care of other chemical pollutants. Another drawback to chemical treatments is the unpleasant taste of the water after it is treated. You can remedy this by adding powdered drink mix to the water. Filters are the preferred method for treating water. Many filters remove Giardia and organic and inorganic contaminants and do not leave an aftertaste. Water filters are far from perfect as they can easily become clogged or leak if a gasket wears out. It is always a good idea to carry a backup supply of chemical treatment tablets in case your filter decides to quit on you.

Food. If we are talking about survival, you can go days without food, as long as you have water. But, we are also talking about comfort. Try to avoid foods that are high in sugar and fat like candy bars and potato chips. These food types are harder to digest and are low in nutritional value. Instead, bring along foods that are easy to pack, nutritious, and high in energy (e.g., bagels, nutrition bars, dehydrated fruit, gorp, and jerky). If you are on an overnight trip, easy-to-fix dinners include rice mixes with dehydrated potatoes, corn, pasta with cheese sauce, and soup mixes. For a tasty breakfast, you can fix hot oatmeal with brown sugar and reconstituted milk powder topped off with banana chips. If you like a hot drink in the morning, bring along herbal tea bags or hot chocolate. If you are a coffee junkie, you can purchase coffee that is packaged like tea bags. You can prepackage all of your meals in heavy-duty resealable plastic bags to keep food from spilling in your pack. These bags can be reused to pack out trash.

Shelter. The type of shelter you choose depends less on the conditions than on your tolerance for discomfort. Shelter comes in many forms—tent, tarp, lean-to, bivy sack, cabin, cave, etc. If you are camping in the desert, a bivy sack may suffice, but if you are above the treeline and a storm is approaching, a better choice is a three- or four-season tent. Tents are the logical and most popular choice for most back-packers as they are lightweight and packable—and you can rest assured that you always have shelter from the elements. Before you leave on your trip, anticipate what the weather and terrain will be like and plan for the type of shelter that will work best for your comfort level (see Equipment later in this section).

Finding a campsite. If there are established campsites, stick to those. If not, start looking for a campsite early—around 3:30 or 4 p.m. Stop at the first decent site you see. Depending on the area, it could be a long time before you find another suitable location. Pitch your camp in an area that is level. Make sure the area is at least 200 feet from fragile areas like lakeshores, meadows, and stream banks. And try to avoid areas thick in underbrush, as they can harbor insects and provide cover for approaching animals.

If you are camping in stormy, rainy weather, look for a rocky outcrop or a shelter in the trees to keep the wind from blowing over your tent all night. Be sure that you do not camp under trees with dead limbs that might break off on top of you. Also, try to find an area that has an absorbent surface, such as sandy soil or forest duff. This, in addition to camping on a surface with a slight angle, will provide better drainage. By all means, do not dig trenches to provide drainage around your tent—remember you are practicing zero-impact camping.

If you are in bear country, steer clear of creekbeds or animal paths. If you see any signs of a bear's presence (i.e., scat or footprints), relocate. You will need to find a campsite near a tall tree where you can hang your food and other items that may attract bears such as deodorant, toothpaste, or soap. Carry a lightweight nylon rope with which to hang your food. As a rule, you should hang your food at least 20 feet from the ground and 5 feet away from the tree trunk. You can put food and other items in a waterproof stuff sack and tie one end of the rope to the stuff sack. To get the other end of the rope over the tree branch, tie a good-sized rock to it, and gently toss the rock over the tree branch. Pull the stuff sack up until it reaches the top of the branch and tie it off securely. Do not hang your food near your tent! If possible, hang your food at least 100 feet away from your campsite. Alternatives to hanging your food are bear-proof plastic tubes and metal bear boxes.

Lastly, think of comfort. Lie down on the ground where you intend to sleep and see if it is a good fit. For morning warmth (and a nice view to wake up to), have your tent face east.

First Aid

I know you are tough, but get 10 miles into the woods and develop a blister and you will wish you had carried that first-aid kit. Face it, it is just plain good sense. Many companies produce lightweight, compact first-aid kits. Just make sure yours contains at least the following:

- adhesive bandages
- moleskin or duct tape
- various sterile gauze and dressings
- white surgical tape
- an Ace bandage
- an antihistamine
- aspirin
- Betadine solution
- a first-aid book
- antacid tablets
- tweezers
- scissors
- antibacterial wipes
- triple antibiotic ointment
- plastic gloves
- sterile cotton tip applicators
- syrup of ipecac (to induce vomiting)
- thermometer
- wire splint

Here are a few tips for dealing with and hopefully preventing certain ailments.

Sunburn. Take along sunscreen or sun block, protective clothing, and a wide-brimmed hat. If you do get a sunburn, treat the area with aloe vera gel, and protect the area from further sun exposure. At higher elevations, the sun's radiation can be particularly damaging to the skin. Remember that your eyes are vulnerable to this radiation as well. Sunglasses can be a good way to prevent headaches and permanent eye damage from the sun, especially in places where light-colored rock or patches of snow reflect light up in your face.

Blisters. Be prepared to take care of these hike-spoilers by carrying moleskin (a lightly padded adhesive), gauze and tape, or adhesive bandages. An effective way to apply moleskin is to cut out a circle of moleskin and remove the center—like a doughnut—and place it over the blistered area. Cutting the center out will reduce the pressure applied to the sensitive skin. Other products can help you combat blisters. Some are applied to suspicious hot spots before a blister forms to help decrease friction to that area, while others are applied to the blister after it has popped to help prevent further irritation.

Insect bites and stings. You can treat most insect bites and stings by applying hydrocortisone 1% cream topically and taking a pain medication such as ibuprofen or acetaminophen to reduce swelling. If you forgot to pack these items, a cold compress or a paste of mud and ashes can sometimes assuage the itching and discomfort. Remove any stingers by using tweezers or scraping the area with your fingernail or a knife blade. Do not pinch the area, as you will only spread the venom.

Some hikers are highly sensitive to bites and stings and may have a serious allergic reaction that can be life-threatening. Symptoms of a serious allergic reaction can include wheezing, an asthmatic attack, and shock. The treatment for this severe type of reaction is epinephrine. If you know that you are sensitive to bites and stings, carry a pre-packaged kit of epinephrine, which can be obtained only by prescription from your doctor.

Ticks. Ticks can carry diseases such as Rocky Mountain spotted fever and Lyme disease. The best defense is, of course, prevention. If you know you are going to be hiking through an area littered with ticks, wear long pants and a long sleeved shirt. You can apply a permethrin repellent to your clothing and a Deet repellent to exposed skin. At the end of your hike, do a spot check for ticks (and insects in general). If you do find a tick, grab the head of the tick firmly—with a pair of tweezers if you have them—and gently pull it away from the skin with a twisting motion. Sometimes the mouth parts linger, embedded in your skin. If this happens, try to remove them with a disinfected needle. Clean the affected area with an antibacterial cleanser and then apply triple antibiotic ointment. Monitor the area for a few days. If irritation persists or a white spot develops, see a doctor for possible infection.

Poison ivy, oak, and sumac. These skin irritants can be found almost anywhere in North America and come in the form of a bush or a vine, having leaflets in groups of three, five, seven, or nine. Learn how to spot the plants. The oil they secrete can cause an allergic reaction in the form of blisters, usually about 12 hours after exposure. The itchy rash can last from ten days to several weeks. The best defense against these irritants is to wear clothing that covers the arms, legs, and torso. For summer, zip-off cargo pants come in handy. There are also non-prescription lotions you can apply to exposed skin that guard against the effects of poison ivy/oak/sumac and can be washed off with soap and water. If you think you were in contact with the plants, after hiking (or even on the trail during longer hikes) wash with soap and water. Taking a hot shower with soap after you return home from your hike will also help to remove any lingering oil from your skin. Should you contract a rash from any of these plants, use an antihistamine to reduce the itching. If the rash is localized, create a light bleach/water wash to dry up the area. If the rash has spread, either tough it out or see your doctor about getting a dose of cortisone (available both orally and by injection).

Snakebites. Snakebites are rare in North America. Unless startled or provoked, the majority of snakes will not bite. If you are wise to their habitats and keep a careful eye on the trail, you should be just fine. When stepping over logs, first step on the log, making sure you can see what is on the other side before stepping down. Though your chances of being struck are slim, it is wise to know what to do in the event you are.

If a *non-poisonous* snake bites you, allow the wound to bleed a small amount and then cleanse the wounded area with a Betadine solution (10% povidone iodine). Rinse the wound with clean water (preferably) or fresh urine (it might sound ugly, but it is sterile). Once the area is clean, cover it with triple antibiotic ointment and a clean bandage. Remember, most residual damage from snakebites, poisonous or otherwise, comes from infection, not the snake's venom. Keep the area as clean as possible and get medical attention immediately.

If somebody in your party is bitten by a poisonous snake, follow these steps:

1. Calm the patient.
2. Remove jewelry, watches, and restrictive clothing, and immobilize the affected limb. Do not elevate the

injury. Medical opinions vary on whether the area should be lower or level with the heart, but the consensus is that it should not be above it.

3. Make a note of the circumference of the limb at the bite site and at various points above the site as well. This will help you monitor swelling.

4. Evacuate your victim. Ideally, he or she should be carried out to minimize movement. If the victim appears to be doing okay, he or she can walk. Stop and rest frequently, and if the swelling appears to be spreading or the patient's symptoms increase, change your plan and find a way to get your patient transported.

5. If you are waiting for rescue, make sure to keep your patient comfortable and hydrated (unless he begins vomiting).

Snakebite treatment is rife with old-fashioned remedies: You used to be told to cut and suck the venom out of the bite site or to use a suction cup extractor for the same purpose; applying an electric shock to the area was even in vogue for a while. Do not do any of these things. Do not apply ice, do not give your patient painkillers, and do not apply a tourniquet. All you really want to do is keep your patient calm and get help. If you are alone and have to hike out, do not run—you will only increase the flow of blood throughout your system. Instead, walk calmly.

Dehydration. Have you ever hiked in hot weather and had a roaring headache and felt fatigued after only a few miles? More than likely you were dehydrated. Symptoms of dehydration include fatigue, headache, and decreased coordination and judgment. When you are hiking, your body's rate of fluid loss depends on the outside temperature, humidity, altitude, and your activity level. On average, a hiker walking in warm weather will lose four liters of fluid a day. That fluid loss is easily replaced by normal consumption of liquids and food. However, if a hiker is walking briskly in hot, dry weather and hauling a heavy pack, he or she can lose one to three liters of water an hour. It is important to always carry plenty of water and to stop often and drink fluids regularly, even if you are not thirsty.

Heat exhaustion is the result of a loss of large amounts of electrolytes and often occurs if a hiker is dehydrated and has been under heavy exertion. Common symptoms of heat exhaustion include cramping, exhaustion, fatigue, lightheadedness, and nausea. You can treat heat exhaustion by getting out of the sun and drinking an electrolyte solution made up of one teaspoon of salt and one tablespoon of sugar dissolved in a liter of water. Drink this solution slowly over a period of 1 hour. Drinking plenty of fluids (preferably an electrolyte solution/sports drink) can prevent heat exhaustion. Avoid hiking during the hottest parts of the day, and wear breathable clothing, a wide-brimmed hat, and sunglasses.

Hypothermia is one of the biggest dangers in the back-country, especially for day hikers in the summertime. That may sound strange, but imagine starting out on a hike in midsummer when it is sunny and 80 degrees out. You are clad in nylon shorts and a cotton T-shirt. About halfway through your hike, the sky begins to cloud up, and in the next hour, a light drizzle begins to fall and the wind starts to pick up. Before you know it, you are soaking wet and shivering—the perfect recipe for hypothermia. More advanced signs include decreased coordination, slurred speech, and blurred vision. When a victim's temperature falls below 92 degrees, the blood pressure and pulse plummet, possibly leading to coma and death.

To avoid hypothermia, always bring a windproof/rainproof shell, a fleece jacket, long underwear made of a breathable, synthetic fiber, gloves, and hat when you are hiking in the mountains. Learn to adjust your clothing layers based on the temperature. If you are climbing uphill at a moderate pace, you will stay warm, but when you stop for a break you will become cold quickly, unless you add more layers of clothing.

If a hiker is showing advanced signs of hypothermia, dress him or her in dry clothes and make sure he or she is wearing a hat and gloves. Place the person in a sleeping bag in a tent or shelter that will protect him or her from the wind and other elements. Give the person warm fluids to drink and keep him awake.

Frostbite. When the mercury dips below 32 degrees, your extremities begin to chill. If a persistent chill attacks a localized area, say, your hands or your toes, the circulatory system reacts by cutting off blood flow to the affected area—the idea being to protect and preserve the body's overall temperature. And so, it is death by attrition for the affected area. Ice crystals start to form from the water in the cells of the neglected tissue. Deprived of heat, nourishment, and now water, the tissue literally starves. This is frostbite.

Prevention is your best defense against this situation. Most prone to frostbite are your face, hands, and feet, so protect these areas well. Wool is the traditional material of choice because it provides ample air space for insulation and draws moisture away from the skin. Synthetic fabrics, however, have made great strides in the cold weather clothing market. Do your research. A pair of light silk liners under your regular gloves is a good trick for keeping warm. They afford some additional warmth, but more importantly, they will allow you to remove your mitts for tedious work without exposing the skin.

If your feet or hands start to feel cold or numb due to the elements, warm them as quickly as possible. Place cold hands under your armpits or bury them in your crotch. If your feet are cold, change your socks. If there is plenty of room in your boots, add another pair of socks. Do remember, though, that constricting your feet in tight boots can restrict blood flow and actually make your feet colder more quickly. Your socks need to have breathing room if they are going to be effective. Dead air provides insulation. If your face is cold, place your warm hands over your face, or simply wear a head stocking.

Should your skin go numb and start to appear white and waxy, chances are you have got or are developing frostbite. Do not try to thaw the area unless you can maintain the warmth. In other words, do not stop to warm up your frostbitten feet only to head back on the trail. You will do more damage than good. Tests have shown that hikers who walked on thawed feet did more harm, and endured more pain, than hikers who left the affected areas alone. Do your best to get out of the cold entirely and seek medical attention—which usually consists of performing a rapid rewarming in water for twenty to thirty minutes.

The overall objective in preventing both hypothermia and frostbite is to keep the body's core warm. Protect key areas where heat escapes, like the top of the head, and maintain the proper nutrition level. Foods that are high in calories aid the body in producing heat. Never smoke or drink when you are in situations where the cold is threatening. By affecting blood flow, these activities ultimately cool the body's core temperature.

Altitude sickness. High lofty peaks, clear alpine lakes, and vast mountain views beckon hikers to the high country.

But those who like to venture high may become victims of altitude sickness (also known as acute mountain sickness—AMS). Altitude sickness is your body's reaction to insufficient oxygen in the blood due to decreased barometric pressure. While some hikers may feel lightheaded, nauseous, and experience shortness of breath at 7,000 feet, others may not experience these symptoms until they reach 10,000 feet or higher.

Slowing your ascent to high places and giving your body a chance to acclimatize to the higher elevations can prevent altitude sickness. For example, if you live at sea level and are planning a weeklong backpacking trip to elevations between 7,000 and 12,000 feet, start by staying below 7,000 feet for one night, then move to between 7,000 and 10,000 feet for another night or two. Avoid strenuous exertion and alcohol to give your body a chance to adjust to the new altitude. It is also important to eat light food and drink plenty of non-alcoholic fluids, preferably water. Loss of appetite at altitude is common, but you must eat!

Most hikers who experience mild to moderate AMS develop a headache and/or nausea, grow lethargic, and have problems sleeping. The treatment for AMS is simple: stop heading uphill. Keep eating and drinking water and take meds for the headache. You actually need to take more breaths at altitude than at sea level, so breathe a little faster without hyperventilating. If symptoms do not improve over 24 to 48 hours, descend. Once a victim descends about 2,000 to 3,000 feet, his signs will usually begin to diminish.

Severe AMS comes in two forms: High altitude pulmonary edema (HAPE) and high altitude cerebral edema (HACE). HAPE, an accumulation of fluid in the lungs, can occur above 8,000 feet. Symptoms include rapid heart rate, shortness of breath at rest, AMS symptoms, dry cough developing into a wet cough, gurgling sounds, flu-like or bronchitis symptoms, and lack of muscle coordination. HAPE is life-threatening, so descend immediately, at least 2,000–4,000 feet. HACE usually occurs above 12,000 feet but sometimes occurs above 10,000 feet. Symptoms are similar to HAPE but also include seizures, hallucinations, paralysis, and vision disturbances. Descend immediately—HACE is also life-threatening.

Hantavirus pulmonary syndrome (HPS). Deer mice spread the virus that causes HPS, and humans contract it from breathing it in, usually when they have disturbed an area with dust and mice feces from nests or surfaces with mice droppings or urine. Exposure to large numbers of rodents and their feces or urine presents the greatest risk. As hikers, we sometimes enter old buildings, and often deer mice live in these places. We may not be around long enough to be exposed, but do be aware of this disease. About half the people who develop HPS die. Symptoms are flu-like and appear about two to three weeks after exposure. After initial symptoms, a dry cough and shortness of breath follow. Breathing is difficult. If you even think you might have HPS, see a doctor immediately!

Natural Hazards

Besides tripping over a rock or tree root on the trail, there are some real hazards to be aware of while hiking. Even if where you are hiking does not have the plethora of poisonous snakes and plants, insects, and grizzly bears found in other parts of the United States, there are a few weather conditions and predators you may need to take into account.

Lightning. Thunderstorms build over the mountains almost every day during the summer. Lightning is generated by thunderheads and can strike without warning, even several miles away from the nearest overhead cloud. The best rule of thumb is to start leaving exposed peaks, ridges, and canyon rims by about noon. This time can vary a little depending on storm buildup. Keep an eye on cloud formation and do not underestimate how fast a storm can build. The bigger they get, the more likely a thunderstorm will happen. Lightning takes the path of least resistance, so if you are the high point, it might choose you. Ducking under a rock overhang is dangerous as you form the shortest path between the rock and ground. If you dash below treeline, avoid standing under the only or the tallest tree. If you are caught above treeline, stay away from anything metal you might be carrying. Move down off the ridge slightly to a low, treeless point and squat until the storm passes. If you have an insulating pad, squat on it. Avoid having both your hands and feet touching the ground at once and never lay flat. If you hear a buzzing sound or feel your hair standing on end, move quickly as an electrical charge is building up.

Flash floods. On July 31, 1976, a torrential downpour unleashed by a thunderstorm dumped tons of water into the Big Thompson watershed near Estes Park. Within hours, a wall of water moved down the narrow canyon killing 139 people and causing more than $30 million in property damage. The spooky thing about flash floods, especially in western canyons, is that they can appear out of nowhere from a storm many miles away. While hiking or driving in canyons, keep an eye on the weather. Always climb to safety if danger threatens. Flash floods usually subside quickly, so be patient and do not cross a swollen stream.

Bears. Most of the United States (outside of the Pacific Northwest and parts of the Northern Rockies) does not have a grizzly bear population, although some rumors exist about sightings where there should be none. Black bears are plentiful, however. Here are some tips in case you and a bear scare each other. Most of all, avoid surprising a bear. Talk or sing where visibility or hearing is limited, such as along a rushing creek or in thick brush. In grizzly country especially, carry bear spray in a holster on your pack belt where you can quickly grab it. While hiking, watch for bear tracks (five toes), droppings (sizable with leaves, partly digested berries, seeds, and/or animal fur), or rocks and roots along the trail that show signs of being dug up (this could be a bear looking for bugs to eat). Keep a clean camp, hang food or use bearproof storage containers, and do not sleep in the clothes you wore while cooking. Be especially careful to avoid getting between a mother and her cubs. In late summer and fall, bears are busy eating to fatten up for winter, so be extra careful around berry bushes and oakbrush. If you do encounter a bear, move away slowly while facing the bear, talk softly, and avoid direct eye contact. Give the bear room to escape. Since bears are very curious, it might stand upright to get a better whiff of you, and it may even charge you to try to intimidate you. Try to stay calm. If a black bear attacks you, fight back with anything you have handy. If a grizzly bear attacks you, your best option is to "play dead" by lying face down on the ground and covering the back of your neck and head with your hands. Unleashed dogs have been known to come running back to their owners with a bear close behind. Keep your dog on a leash or leave it at home.

Mountain lions. Mountain lions appear to be getting more comfortable around humans as long as deer (their favorite prey) are in an area with adequate cover. Usually elusive and quiet, lions rarely attack people. If you meet a lion, give it a chance to escape. Stay calm and talk firmly to it. Back away slowly while facing the lion. If you run, you will only encourage the cat to chase you. Make yourself look large by opening a jacket, if you have one, or waving your hiking poles. If the lion behaves aggressively, throw stones, sticks, or whatever you can while remaining tall. If a lion does attack, fight for your life with anything you can grab.

Moose. Because moose have very few natural predators, they do not fear humans like other animals. You might find moose in sagebrush and wetter areas of willow, aspen, and pine, or in beaver habitats. Mothers with calves, as well as bulls during mating season, can be particularly aggressive. If a moose threatens you, back away slowly and talk calmly to it. Keep your pets away from moose.

Other considerations. Hunting is a popular sport in the United States, especially during rifle season in October and November. Hiking is still enjoyable in those months in many areas, so just take a few precautions. First, learn when the different hunting seasons start and end in the area in which you will be hiking. During this time frame, be sure to wear at least a blaze orange hat and possibly put an orange vest over your pack. Do not be surprised to see hunters in camo outfits carrying bows or rifles around during their season. If you would feel more comfortable without hunters around, hike in national parks and monuments or state and local parks where hunting is not allowed.

Navigation

Whether you are going on a short hike in a familiar area or planning a weeklong backpack trip, you should always be equipped with the proper navigational equipment—at the very least a detailed map and a sturdy compass.

Maps. There are many different types of maps available to help you find your way on the trail. Easiest to find are Forest Service maps and Bureau of Land Management (BLM) maps. These maps tend to cover large areas, so be sure they are detailed enough for your particular trip. You can also obtain National Park maps as well as high-quality maps from private companies and trail groups. These maps can be obtained either from outdoor stores or from ranger stations.

US Geological Survey (USGS) topographic maps are particularly popular with hikers—especially serious backcountry hikers. These maps contain the standard map symbols such as roads, lakes, and rivers, as well as contour lines that show the details of the trail terrain like ridges, valleys, passes, and mountain peaks. The 7.5-minute series (1 inch on the map equals approximately 2/5 of a mile on the ground) provides the closest inspection available. USGS maps are available by mail (US Geological Survey, Map Distribution Branch, PO Box 25286, Denver, CO 80225) or at mapping. usgs.gov/esic/to_order.html.

If you want to check out the high-tech world of maps, you can purchase topographic maps on CD-ROMs. These mapping software let you select a route on your computer, print it out, then take it with you on the trail. Some mapping software let you insert symbols and labels, download waypoints from a GPS unit, and export the maps to other software programs.

The art of map reading is a skill that you can develop by first practicing in an area you are familiar with. To begin, orient the map so the map is lined up in the correct direction (i.e. north on the map is lined up with true north). Next, familiarize yourself with the map symbols and try and match them up with terrain features around you such as a high ridge, mountain peak, river, or lake. If you are practicing with a USGS map, notice the contour lines. On gentler terrain, these contour lines are spaced farther apart, and on steeper terrain they are closer together. Pick a short loop trail, and stop frequently to check your position on the map. As you practice map reading, you will learn how to anticipate a steep section on the trail or a good place to take a rest break, and so on.

Compasses. First off, the sun is not a substitute for a compass. So, what kind of compass should you have? Here are some characteristics you should look for: a rectangular base with detailed scales, a liquid-filled housing, protective housing, a sighting line on the mirror, luminous alignment and back-bearing arrows, a luminous north-seeking arrow, and a well-defined bezel ring.

You can learn compass basics by reading the detailed instructions included with your compass. If you want to fine-tune your compass skills, sign up for an orienteering class or purchase a book on compass-reading. Once you have learned the basic skills of using a compass, remember to practice these skills before you head into the backcountry.

If you are a klutz at using a compass, you may be interested in checking out the technical wizardry of the GPS device. The GPS was developed by the Pentagon and works off twenty-four NAVSTAR satellites, which were designed to guide missiles to their targets. A GPS device is a handheld unit that calculates your latitude and longitude with the easy press of a button. The Department of Defense used to scramble the satellite signals a bit to prevent civilians (and spies!) from getting extremely accurate readings, but that practice was discontinued in May 2000, and GPS units now provide nearly pinpoint accuracy (within 30 to 60 feet).

There are many different types of GPS units available, and they range in price from $100 to $400. In general, all GPS units have a display screen and keypad where you input information. In addition to acting as a compass, the unit allows you to plot your route, easily retrace your path, track your travelling speed, find the mileage between waypoints, and calculate the total mileage of your route.

Before you purchase a GPS unit, keep in mind that these devices do not pick up signals indoors, in heavily wooded areas, on mountain peaks, or in deep valleys. Also, batteries can wear out or other technical problems can develop. A GPS unit should be used in conjunction with a map and compass, not in place of those items.

Pedometers. A pedometer is a small clip-on unit with a digital display that calculates your hiking distance in miles or kilometers based on your walking stride. Some units also calculate the calories you burn and your total hiking time. Pedometers are available at most large outdoor stores and range in price from $20 to $40.

Trip Planning

Planning your hiking adventure begins with letting a friend or relative know your trip itinerary so they can call for help if you do not return at your scheduled time. Your next task is to make sure you are outfitted to experience the risks and rewards of the trail. This section highlights gear and clothing you may want to take with you to get the most out of your hike.

Day Hikes

- bear repellent spray (if hiking in grizzly country)
- camera
- compass/GPS unit
- pedometer
- daypack
- first-aid kit
- food
- guidebook
- headlamp/flashlight with extra batteries and bulbs
- hat
- insect repellent
- knife/multipurpose tool
- map
- matches in waterproof container and fire starter
- fleece jacket
- rain gear
- space blanket
- sunglasses
- sunscreen
- swimsuit and/or fishing gear (if hiking to a lake)
- watch
- water
- water bottles/water hydration system

Overnight Trip

- backpack and waterproof rain cover
- backpacker's trowel
- bandanna

- bear repellent spray (if hiking in grizzly country)
- bear bell
- biodegradable soap
- pot scrubber
- collapsible water container (2–3 gallon capacity)
- clothing—extra wool socks, shirt and shorts
- cook set/utensils
- ditty bags to store gear
- extra plastic resealable bags
- gaiters
- garbage bag
- ground cloth
- journal/pen
- nylon rope to hang food
- long underwear
- permit (if required)
- rain jacket and pants
- sandals to wear around camp and to ford streams
- sleeping bag
- waterproof stuff sack
- sleeping pad
- small bath towel
- stove and fuel
- tent
- toiletry items
- water filter
- whistle

With the outdoor market currently flooded with products, many of which are pure gimmickry, it seems impossible to both differentiate and choose. Do I really need a tropical-fish-lined collapsible shower? (No, you do not.) The only defense against the maddening quantity of items thrust in your face is to think practically—and to do so before you go shopping. The worst buys are impulsive buys. Since most name brands will differ only slightly in quality, it is best to know what you are looking for in terms of function. Buy only what you need. You will, do not forget, be carrying what you have bought on your back. Here are some things to keep in mind before you go shopping.

Clothes. Clothing is your armor against Mother Nature's little surprises. Hikers should be prepared for any possibility, especially when hiking in mountainous areas. Adequate rain protection and extra layers of clothing are a good idea. In summer, a wide-brimmed hat can help keep the sun at bay. In the winter months, the first layer you will want to wear is a "wicking" layer of long underwear that keeps perspiration away from your skin. Wear long underwear made from synthetic fibers that wick moisture away from the skin and draw it toward the next layer of clothing, where it then evaporates. Avoid wearing long underwear made of cotton as it is slow to dry and keeps moisture next to your skin.

The second layer you will wear is the "insulating" layer. Aside from keeping you warm, this layer needs to "breathe" so you stay dry while hiking. A fabric that provides insulation and dries quickly is fleece. It is interesting to note that this one-of-a-kind fabric is made out of recycled plastic.

Purchasing a zip-up jacket made of this material is highly recommended.

The last line of layering defense is the "shell" layer. You will need some type of waterproof, windproof, breathable jacket that will fit over all of your other layers. It should have a large hood that fits over a hat. You will also need a good pair of rain pants made from a similar waterproof, breathable fabric. Some Gore-Tex jackets cost as much as $500, but you should know that there are more affordable fabrics out there that work just as well.

Now that you have learned the basics of layering, you cannot forget to protect your hands and face. In cold, windy, or rainy weather, you will need a hat made of wool or fleece and insulated, waterproof gloves that will keep your hands warm and toasty. As mentioned earlier, buying an additional pair of light silk liners to wear under your regular gloves is a good idea.

Footwear. If you have any extra money to spend on your trip, put that money into boots or trail shoes. Poor shoes will bring a hike to a halt faster than anything else. To avoid this annoyance, buy shoes that provide support and are light-weight and flexible. A lightweight hiking boot is better than a heavy leather mountaineering boot for most day hikes and backpacking. Trail running shoes provide a little extra cushion and are made in a high-top style that many people wear for hiking. These running shoes are lighter, more flexible, and more breathable than hiking boots. If you know you will be hiking in wet weather often, purchase boots or shoes with a Gore-Tex liner, which will help keep your feet dry.

When buying your boots, be sure to wear the same type of socks you will be wearing on the trail. If the boots you are buying are for cold-weather hiking, try the boots on while wearing two pairs of socks. Speaking of socks, a good cold-weather sock combination is to wear a thinner sock made of wool or polypropylene covered by a heavier outer sock made of wool or a synthetic/wool mix. The inner sock protects the foot from the rubbing effects of the outer sock and prevents blisters. Many outdoor stores have some type of ramp to simulate hiking uphill and downhill. Be sure to take advantage of this test, as toe-jamming boot fronts can be very painful and debilitating on the downhill trek.

Once you have purchased your footwear, be sure to break them in before you hit the trail. New footwear is often stiff and needs to be stretched and molded to your foot.

Hiking poles. Hiking poles help with balance and more importantly take pressure off your knees. The ones with shock absorbers are easier on your elbows and knees. Some poles even come with a camera attachment to be used as a monopod. And heaven forbid you meet a mountain lion, bear, or unfriendly dog, the poles can make you look a lot bigger.

Backpacks. No matter what type of hiking you do, you will need a pack of some sort to carry the basic trail essentials. There are a variety of backpacks on the market, but let us first discuss what you intend to use it for. Day hikes or overnight trips?

If you plan on doing a day hike, a daypack should have some of the following characteristics: a padded hip belt that is at least 2 inches in diameter (avoid packs with only a small nylon piece of webbing for a hip belt); a chest strap (the chest strap helps stabilize the pack against your body); external pockets to carry water and other items that you want easy access to; an internal pocket to hold keys, a knife, a wallet, and other miscellaneous items; an external lashing system to hold a jacket; and, if you so desire, a hydration pocket for carrying a hydration system (which consists of a water bladder with an attachable drinking hose).

For short hikes, some hikers like to use a fanny pack to store just a camera, food, a compass, a map, and other trail essentials. Most fanny packs have pockets for two water bottles and a padded hip belt.

If you intend to do an extended, overnight trip, there are multiple considerations. First off, you need to decide what kind of framed pack you want. There are two backpack types for backpacking: the internal frame and the external frame. An internal frame pack rests closer to your body, making it more stable and easier to balance when hiking over rough terrain. An external frame pack is just that, an aluminum frame attached to the exterior of the pack. Some hikers consider an external frame pack to be better for long backpack trips because it distributes the pack weight better and allows you to carry heavier loads. It is often easier to pack, and your gear is more accessible. It also offers better back ventilation in hot weather.

The most critical measurement for fitting a pack is torso length. The pack needs to rest evenly on your hips without sagging. A good pack will come in two or three sizes and have straps and hip belts that are adjustable according to your body size and characteristics.

When you purchase a backpack, go to an outdoor store with salespeople who are knowledgeable in how to properly fit a pack. Once the pack is fitted for you, load the pack with the amount of weight you plan on taking on the trail. The weight of the pack should be distributed evenly and you should be able to swing your arms and walk briskly without feeling out of balance. Another good technique for evaluating a pack is to walk up and down stairs and make quick turns to the right and to the left to be sure the pack does not feel out of balance. Other features that are nice to have on a backpack include a removable daypack or fanny pack, external pockets for extra water, and extra lash points to attach a jacket or other items.

Sleeping bags and pads. Sleeping bags are rated by temperature. You can purchase a bag made with synthetic insulation, or you can buy a goose down bag. Goose down bags are more expensive, but they have a higher insulating capacity by weight and will keep their loft longer. You will want to purchase a bag with a temperature rating that fits the time of year and conditions you are most likely to camp in. One caveat: The techno-standard for temperature ratings is far from perfect. Ratings vary from manufacturer to manufacturer, so to protect yourself, you should purchase a bag rated 10–15 degrees below the temperature you expect to be camping in. Synthetic bags are more resistant to water than down bags, but many down bags are now made with a Gore-Tex shell that helps to repel water. Down bags are also more compressible than synthetic bags and take up less room in your pack, which is an important consideration if you are planning a multiday backpack trip. Features to look for in a sleeping bag include a mummy style bag, a hood you can cinch down around your head in cold weather, and draft tubes along the zippers that help keep heat in and drafts out.

You will also want a sleeping pad to provide insulation and padding from the cold ground. There are different types of sleeping pads available, from the more expensive self-inflating air mattresses to the less expensive closed-cell foam pads. Self-inflating air mattresses are usually heavier than closed-cell foam mattresses and are prone to punctures.

Tents. The tent is your home away from home while on the trail. It provides protection from wind, rain, snow, and insects. A three-season tent is a good choice for back-packing and can range in price from $100 to $500. These lightweight and versatile tents provide protection in all types of weather, except heavy snowstorms or high winds, and range in weight from four to eight pounds. Look for a tent that is easy to set up and will easily fit two people with gear. Dome-type tents usually offer more headroom and places to store gear. Other handy tent features include a vestibule where you can store wet boots and backpacks. Some nice-to-have items in a tent include interior pockets to store small items and lashing points to hang a clothesline. Most three-season tents also come with stakes so you can secure the tent in high winds. Before you purchase a tent, set it up and take it down a few times to be sure it is easy to handle. Also, sit inside the tent and make sure it has enough room for you and your gear.

Cell phones. Many hikers are carrying their cell phones into the backcountry these days in case of emergency. That is fine and good, but please know that cell phone coverage is often poor to non-existent in valleys, canyons, and thick forest. More importantly, people have started to call for help because they are tired or lost. Let us go back to being pre-pared. You are responsible for yourself in the backcountry. Use your brain to avoid problems, and if you do encounter one, first use your brain to try to correct the situation. Only use your cell phone, if it works, in true emergencies. If it does not work down low in a valley, try hiking to a high point where you might get reception.

Hiking with Children

Hiking with children is not a matter of how many miles you can cover or how much elevation gain you make in a day; it is about seeing and experiencing nature through their eyes.

Kids like to explore and have fun. They like to stop and point out bugs and plants, look under rocks, jump in puddles, and throw sticks. If you are taking a toddler or young child on a hike, start with a trail that you are familiar with. Trails that have interesting things for kids, like piles of leaves to play in or a small stream to wade through during the summer, will make the hike much more enjoyable for them and will keep them from getting bored.

You can keep your child's attention if you have a strategy before starting on the trail. Using games is not only an effective way to keep a child's attention, but is also a great way to teach him or her about nature. Quiz children on the names of plants and animals. Pick up a family-friendly outdoor hobby like Geocaching (www.geocaching.com) or Letterboxing (www.atlasquest.com), both of which combine the outdoors, clue solving, and treasure hunting. If your children are old enough, let them carry their own daypack filled with snacks and water. So that you are sure to go at their pace and not yours, let them lead the way. Playing follow the leader works particularly well when you have a group of children. Have each child take a turn at being the leader.

With children, a lot of clothing is key. The only thing predictable about weather is that it will change. Especially in mountainous areas, weather can change dramatically in a very short time. Always bring extra clothing for children, regardless of the season. In the winter, have your children wear wool socks and warm layers such as long underwear, a fleece jacket and hat, wool mittens, and good rain gear. It is not a bad idea to have these along in late fall and early spring as well. Good footwear is also important. A sturdy pair of high-top tennis shoes or lightweight hiking boots is the best bet for little ones. If you are hiking in the summer near a lake or stream, bring along a pair of old sneakers that your child can put on when he wants to go exploring in the water. Remember when you are near any type of water, always watch your child at all times. Also, keep a close eye on teething toddlers who may decide a rock or poison oak leaf is an interesting item to put in their mouth.

From spring through fall, you will want your kids to wear a wide-brimmed hat to keep their face, head, and ears protected from the hot sun. Also, make sure your children wear sunscreen at all times. Choose a brand without PABA—children have sensitive skin and may have an allergic reaction to sunscreen that contains PABA. If you are hiking with a child younger than six months, do not use sunscreen or insect repellent. Instead, be sure that their head, face, neck, and ears are protected from the sun with a wide-brimmed hat and that all other skin exposed to the sun is protected with the appropriate clothing.

Remember that food is fun. Kids like snacks, so it is important to bring a lot of munchies for the trail. Stopping often for snack breaks is a fun way to keep the trail interesting. Raisins, apples, granola bars, crackers and cheese, cereal, and trail mix all make great snacks. Also, a few of their favorite candy treats can go a long way toward heading off a fit of fussing. If your child is old enough to carry his or her own backpack, let him or her fill it with some lightweight "comfort" items such as a doll, a small stuffed animal, or a little toy (you will have to draw the line at bringing the ten-pound

Tonka truck). If your kids do not like drinking water, you can bring some powdered drink mix or a juice box.

Avoid poorly designed child-carrying packs—you do not want to break your back carrying your child. Most child-carrying backpacks designed to hold a forty-pound child will contain a large carrying pocket to hold diapers and other items. Some have an optional rain/sun hood.

Hiking with Your Dog

Bringing your furry friend with you is always more fun than leaving him behind. Our canine pals make great trail buddies because they never complain and always make good company. Hiking with your dog can be a rewarding experience, especially if you plan ahead.

Getting your dog in shape. Before you plan outdoor adventures with your dog, make sure he is in shape for the trail. Getting your dog into shape takes the same discipline as getting yourself into shape, but luckily, your dog can get in shape with you. Take your dog with you on your daily runs or walks. If there is a park near your house, hit a tennis ball or play Frisbee with your dog.

Swimming is also an excellent way to get your dog into shape. If there is a lake or river near where you live and your dog likes the water, have him retrieve a tennis ball or stick. Gradually build your dog's stamina up over a two- to three-month period. A good rule of thumb is to assume that your dog will travel twice as far as you will on the trail. If you plan to do a 5-mile hike, be sure your dog is in shape for a 10-mile hike.

Training your dog for the trail. Before you go on your first hiking adventure with your dog, be sure he has a firm grasp on the basics of canine etiquette and behavior. Make sure he can sit, lie down, stay, and come. One of the most important commands you can teach your canine pal is to "come" under any situation. It is easy for your friend's nose to lead him astray or possibly get lost. Another helpful command is the "get behind" command. When you are on a hiking trail that is narrow, you can have your dog follow behind you when other trail users approach. Nothing is more bothersome than an enthusiastic dog that runs back and forth on the trail and disrupts the peace of the trail for others—or, worse, jumps up on other hikers and gets them muddy. When you see other trail users approaching you on the trail, give them the right of way by quietly stepping off the trail and making your dog lie down and stay until they pass.

Equipment. The most critical pieces of equipment you can invest in for your dog are proper identification and a sturdy leash. Flexi-leads work well for hiking because they give your dog more freedom to explore but still leave you in control. Make sure your dog has identification that includes your name and address and a number for your veterinarian. Other forms of identification for your dog include a tattoo or a microchip. You should consult your veterinarian for more information on these last two options.

The next piece of equipment you will want to consider is a pack for your dog. By no means should you hold all of your dog's essentials in your pack—let him carry his own gear! Dogs that are in good shape can carry 30–40 percent of their own weight.

Most packs are fitted by a dog's weight and girth measurement. Companies that make dog packs generally include guidelines to help you pick out the size that is right for your dog.

Some characteristics to look for when purchasing a pack for your dog include a harness that contains two padded girth straps, a padded chest strap, leash attachments, removable saddlebags, internal water bladders, and external gear cords.

You can introduce your dog to the pack by first placing the empty pack on his back and letting him wear it around the yard. Keep an eye on him during this first introduction. He may decide to chew through the straps if you are not watching him closely. Once he learns to treat the pack as an object of fun and not a foreign enemy, fill the pack evenly on both sides with a few ounces of dog food in resealable plastic bags. Have your dog wear his pack on your daily walks for a period of two to three weeks. Each week, add a little more weight to the pack until your dog will accept carrying the maximum amount of weight he can carry.

You can also purchase collapsible water and dog food bowls for your dog. These bowls are lightweight and can easily be stashed into your pack or your dog's. If you are hiking on rocky terrain or in the snow, you can purchase footwear for your dog that will protect his feet from cuts and bruises.

Always carry plastic bags to remove feces from the trail. It is a courtesy to other trail users and helps protect local wildlife.

The following is a list of items to bring when you take your dog hiking: collapsible water bowls, a comb, a collar and a leash, dog food, plastic bags for feces, a dog pack, flea/tick powder, paw protection, water, and a first-aid kit that contains eye ointment, tweezers, scissors, stretchy foot wrap, gauze, antibacterial wash, sterile cotton tip applicators, antibiotic ointment, and cotton wrap.

First aid for your dog. Your dog is just as prone—if not more prone—to getting in trouble on the trail as you are, so be prepared. Here is a rundown of the more likely misfortunes that might befall your little friend.

Bees and wasps. If a bee or wasp stings your dog, remove the stinger with a pair of tweezers and place a mudpack or a cloth dipped in cold water over the affected area.

Porcupines. One good reason to keep your dog on a leash is to prevent it from getting a nose full of porcupine quills. You may be able to remove the quills with pliers, but a veterinarian is the best person to do this nasty job because most dogs need to be sedated.

Heat stroke. Avoid hiking with your dog in really hot weather. Dogs with heat stroke will pant excessively, lie down and refuse to get up, and become lethargic and disoriented. If your dog shows any of these signs on the trail, have him lie down in the shade. If you are near a stream, pour cool water over your dog's entire body to help bring his body temperature back to normal.

Heartworm. Dogs get heartworms from mosquitoes which carry the disease in the prime mosquito months of July and August. Giving your dog a monthly pill prescribed by your veterinarian easily prevents this condition.

Plant pitfalls. One of the biggest plant hazards for dogs on the trail are foxtails. Foxtails are pointed grass seed heads that bury themselves in your friend's fur, between his toes, and even get in his ear canal. If left unattended, these nasty seeds can work their way under the skin and cause abscesses and other problems. If you have a long-haired dog, consider trimming the hair between his toes and giving him a summer haircut to help prevent foxtails from attaching to his fur. After every hike, always look over your dog for these seeds—especially between his toes and his ears.

Other plant hazards include burrs, thorns, thistles, and poison oak. If you find any burrs or thistles on your dog, remove them as soon as possible before they become an unmanageable mat. Thorns can pierce a dog's foot and cause a great deal of pain. If you see that your dog is lame, stop and check his feet for thorns. Dogs are immune to poison oak, but they can pick up the sticky, oily substance from the plant and transfer it to you.

Protect those paws. Be sure to keep your dog's nails trimmed so he avoids getting soft tissue or joint injuries. If your dog slows and refuses to go on, check to see that his paws are not torn or worn. You can protect your dog's paws from trail hazards such as sharp gravel, foxtails, lava scree, and thorns by purchasing dog boots.

Sunburn. If your dog has light skin, he is an easy target for sunburn on his nose and other exposed skin areas. You can apply a non-toxic sunscreen to exposed skin areas that will help protect him from overexposure to the sun.

Ticks and fleas. Ticks can easily give your dog Lyme disease, as well as other diseases. Before you hit the trail, treat your dog with a flea and tick spray or powder. You can also ask your veterinarian about a once-a-month pour-on treatment that repels fleas and ticks.

Mosquitoes and deer flies. These little flying machines can do a job on your dog's snout and ears. Best bet is to spray your dog with fly repellent for horses to discourage both pests.

Giardia. Dogs can get giardia, which results in diarrhea. It is usually not debilitating, but it is definitely messy. A vaccine against giardia is available.

Mushrooms. Make sure your dog does not sample mushrooms along the trail. They could be poisonous to him, but he does not know that.

When you are finally ready to hit the trail with your dog, keep in mind that national parks and many wilderness areas do not allow dogs on trails. Your best bet is to hike in national forests, BLM lands, and state parks. Always call ahead to see what the restrictions are.

About the Author

Brett Prettyman is a lifelong resident of Utah. He grew up exploring the northern part of the state and did not spend any real time in southern Utah until his late teenage years. He has been trying to make up for it ever since. Brett worked at the *Salt Lake Tribune* for nearly 25 years as the outdoors editor and columnist. Capitol Reef is a favorite family camping and hiking destination for Brett's family—particularly in the fall.

Other FalconGuides from Brett Prettyman:

Fishing Utah

Hiking Utah's High Uintas (revision)